How To Improve Your School

How To Improve Your School

Giving Pupils A Voice

Jean Rudduck and Julia Flutter

continuum
LONDON • NEW YORK

CONTINUUM

The Tower Building, 11 York Road   15 East 26th Street
London SE1 7NX   Suite 1703, New York
UK   NY 10010, USA

www.continuumbooks.com

British Library Cataloguing-in-Publication Data
A catalogue record for this book is available from the British Library.

ISBN 0–8264–6530–7 (hardback)
    0–8264–6531–5 (paperback)

Typeset by Waverley Typesetters, Galashiels
Printed and bound in Great Britain by MPG Books, Bodmin

'It is time that we count students among those with the authority to participate both in the critique and in the reform of education.'

'This call to authorise student perspectives is a call to count students among those who have the knowledge and the position to shape what counts.'

(Cook-Sather, 2002, p. 3)

Contents

Foreword

> Intrigued by this patch of colour or that scent, beguiled by a pretty shape or blown sideways by a wayward breeze, I flit from book to book, subject to subject, place to place; and it is only later, in solitude, that I begin the laborious process of changing it all into something else.
>
> Pullman, P. (2002) *Dreaming of Spires*,
> the *Guardian Review*, 27 July 2002

Well. It wasn't *exactly* like that – but there are some similarities! This book is not reporting a single study; it doesn't move in a stately way from research design through to findings. What we wanted to do was create a picture of the potential of pupil voice to effect change in the way we think about young people and schools. In the last few years pupil voice has developed at an amazing – and somewhat alarming – rate (some of the reasons for this are explored in the book): from diverse small-scale and relatively uncoordinated initiatives it now has a national profile and a national legitimacy.

We have worked across data from various interview-based projects, all with pupil voice at their centre, which we have been involved in since the early 1990s. Because of this it is not easy, without weighing down the text with wearisome notes, to reference all the project sources, but they are listed in the Appendix. Where data are quoted that have not already appeared in print, we refer to these as 'fieldnotes' (e.g. 'Nick Brown's fieldnotes') and information about these sources is also included in the Appendix.

There is still much to learn from pupils about teaching and learning in schools. In this book we did not set out 'to map and conquer the world' (Bob Stake's words) but merely 'to sophisticate the beholding of it'.

Some of the issues that are not covered in this book (for instance, student-as-researcher initiatives, different ways of consulting pupils) will be covered in the following publications – all outcomes of our ESRC Project, *Consulting Pupils about Teaching and Learning*:

Arnot, M., McIntyre, D., Pedder, D., and Reay, D. (2003) *Consultation in the Classroom: Developing Dialogue about Teaching and Learning*, Cambridge: Pearson Publishing.

Fielding, M. and Bragg, S. (2003) *Students as Researchers: Making a Difference*, Cambridge: Pearson Publishing.

Flutter, J., and Rudduck, J. (2004) *Consulting Pupils: What's in it for Schools?* London: Routledge Falmer.

MacBeath, J., Demetriou, H., Rudduck, J. and Myers, K. (2003), *Consulting Pupils: A Toolkit for Teachers*, Cambridge: Pearson Publishing.

Finally, a comment on terms: the word 'student' is gaining ground in secondary schools, although primary school teachers still tend to use the word pupil or child; naming can provoke strong feelings and so we have used both terms, somewhat arbitrarily – a practice that will probably incite even stronger feelings! The book is about 'young people' in school.

JEAN RUDDUCK and JULIA FLUTTER
April 2003

Acknowledgements

We want to thank all the teachers and the pupils, from primary and secondary schools up and down the country, who talked about their work and how they saw the world of school.

We also want to thank the colleagues who, in a succession of pupil voice projects, have helped to move our understanding forward (see Appendix) – and in particular the colleagues who worked with us on two projects funded by the Economic and Social Research Council (ESRC): Susan Harris, Gwen Wallace and, initially, David Gillborn (the *Making Your Way through Secondary School Project, 1991–4*); and Madeleine Arnot, Sara Bragg, Nick Brown, Helen Demetriou, Michael Fielding, Caroline Lanskey, John MacBeath, Donald McIntyre, Kate Myers, David Pedder, Diane Reay and Beth Wang (the *Consulting Pupils about Teaching and Learning Project, 2000–3*).

And a very special thank you to Nichola Daily and Ann Curtis who have helped in so many ways – and always with remarkable patience and good humour.

Preface

This book by Jean Rudduck and Julia Flutter launches the new *Improving Schools* series by Continuum Books. The main aim of this new series is to combine the highest quality academic research with insights from those working within schools and for schools. It is anticipated that the combination of practitioner and academic insights will offer unique and alternative perspectives on important school improvement themes. To date, many school improvement books have not adequately integrated the voices and views of teachers, parents and pupils. In their search for solutions to improving schools they have tended to ignore those most familiar with the terrain. This is certainly not a criticism that can be made of Jean Rudduck and her colleagues as their research and writing have consistently and eloquently captured, reflected and represented the voices of pupils and teachers over many years. Since her early work with the Humanities Curriculum Project, Jean Rudduck has been committed to listening to, and learning from, teachers and pupils. In her classic book *School Improvement: What Can Pupils Tell Us?* she reminded readers of the core purpose of improving schools and of the main recipients of all school improvement efforts – the pupils.

This book is a timely and important because once again it focuses our attention on those most affected by changes in education policy and systems. It draws upon empirical evidence from a number of research projects and distils this into a compelling account of contemporary schooling through the eyes of pupils. This provides a perspective on pervasive structures and practices so familiar that they often cease to be visible and therefore remain substantially unchallenged. The book calls most powerfully for a shift in the way we currently view young people in schools and sets out a case for rethinking aspects of schooling to match our change in perceptions.

The central argument of the book is that we need to see pupils differently, to re-assess their capabilities and to review and change aspects of school organization, relationship and practices to reflect what young people are capable of being and doing. To this end, it is suggested that we need to take seriously what pupils can tell us about their experiences of being a learner in school, about what gets in the way of being a learner and what helps them learn. Moreover, it implies that we need to find ways of involving pupils more closely in the decision-making that affects their lives in school. All too often pupils are left out of the equation when decisions are being made that directly affect them. Reconfiguring relationships with pupils articulates powerfully with important current agendas on constructivist learning and the experience (rather than the teaching) of citizenship.

In this book, pupils' voices are heard and they provide poignant, thoughtful and sometimes haunting insights into their experiences in school. Their reflections upon issues of transition, on teaching and learning and on the way school affects their self-esteem get right to the heart of the problems that still persist within the schooling system. They present their reality and day-to-day experiences of a system that continues to differentiate on the basis of ability or class, of schools considered to be 'good' or 'bad', stacking the odds against some pupils at a very early age. They don't talk about inequity, disadvantage or social barriers, but these themes lie beneath the frustration, cynicism and hopelessness of some of the comments of those young people destined to leave school without achieving success in academic terms.

On a more positive note the pupils' voices also offer rich insights into effective teaching practices and thoughtful accounts of how they learn best. As 'expert witnesses' they provide views on the conditions of learning which enable alternatives to be contemplated as the first step in fundamental change. The sub-text of these rich and engaging accounts is that the pupil voices are important and, if listened to, can be transformative. Listening to pupils means changing the ways teachers and pupils interact and there is evidence from the TLRP/ESRC 'Consulting Pupils Project' that hearing pupils talk about teaching and learning can be a catalyst for change. It is suggested here that genuine consultation and the enhanced participation of young people provide a broader frame for valuing pupil achievement.

The opportunity for developing more democratic and collaborative relationships can transform teaching and learning practices and, perhaps, the whole education system for the better.

The book concludes by arguing that the transformative potential of consulting pupils is considerable. This view is reiterated by others:

> What surprised us most about the pupils was how insightful they were and how fluent many were . . . at expressing their ideas. What surprised *them* most was that anybody was prepared to listen. (Osborne and Collins, 1999).

It is important in the academic world that we also have researchers who are prepared to listen to pupils, and represent their views. This book is important not only because it does this so well, but also because it makes us rethink, revaluate and re-assess exactly what we mean by school improvement. *Who* is it for? The books that follow in this series will present similar challenges to the conventional wisdom about school improvement from both an academic and practitioner perspective. We need new perspectives, new understandings and new insights to move the school improvement field forward and to transform the conditions of learning for all in schools. This book and this series offer an initial step in that direction.

ALMA HARRIS and JANE MCGREGOR

1 Introduction: The Case for Changing Our Perceptions Of Young People

'It were right good. They treated you like adults.' This 14-year-old boy, interviewed soon after he returned to school, was talking about his period of work experience. It is not an unusual response. Nor is the surprise of teachers that students can seem 'totally different' on work experience. Wanting to be treated 'like an adult' is shorthand for a number of aspirations to do with what we have called the 'conditions of learning' in school: in particular the need for respect, responsibility, challenge, support. It is not a new plea but it is one that we need to give serious attention to.

Out of school, many young people find themselves involved in complex relationships and situations, whether within the family or the peer group. Many carry tough responsibilities, balancing multiple roles and often finding themselves dealing with conflicting loyalties. In contrast, the structures of secondary schooling offer, on the whole, less responsibility and autonomy than many young people are accustomed to in their lives outside school. And, compared with TV soaps and youth magazines, there are fewer occasions when anxieties and aspirations can be opened up and explored. The traditional exclusion of young people from the processes of dialogue and decision-making, this bracketing out of their voice, is founded upon an outdated view of childhood which fails to acknowledge young people's capacity to take initiatives and to reflect on issues affecting their lives. In many schools expectations are still shaped by what Gerald Grace calls 'an ideology of immaturity' (1995, p. 202).

A central strand in the argument of this book is that some pupils disengage because the conditions of learning in school today do not always support the development of *all* young people as learners. Indeed, schools have changed less in their deep structures in the last 20 or 30 years than young people have changed. As Sonia Nieto says (1994, pp. 395, 396): 'Educating students today is a far different and more complex proposition than it has been in the past.' Being in school, said Aries (1962), is like being put in quarantine for a number of years – a limbo world between infancy and adulthood. And each time the school leaving age is raised, so the period during which young people remain as 'uneasy, stranded beings' (H. and P. Silver, 1997, p. 5) becomes longer.

We are battling not only with the legacy of the past which constrains our view of what schools and young people might be but also with a set of powerful contemporary initiatives that limit the possibilities for change by defining achievement narrowly and by keeping schools on a tight rein.

This book is an attempt to sketch out the case for changing our perceptions of young people in school and re-thinking aspects of schooling to match our new perceptions. Our argument is that we need

- to see pupils differently and to re-assess their capabilities; and
- to review and change aspects of school organization, relation-ships and practices to reflect what young people are capable of being and doing.

To this end, we should

- take seriously what pupils can tell us about their experience of being a learner in school – about what gets in the way of their learning and what helps them to learn; and
- find ways of involving pupils more closely in decisions that affect their lives in school, whether at the level of the classroom or the institution.

It is important to know what pupils think will make a difference to their commitment to learning and, in turn, to their progress and achievement. We also need to understand more about why we haven't in the past paid much attention to the views of pupils and why it may be important to do so now.

We start by looking at young people today and the images of childhood that schools have traditionally responded to and, to a large extent, reproduced; we then look briefly at the forces that have shaped schools and their expectations of young people as learners.

Young People and Schools

A closer look at young people

In the 1980s M. D. A. Freeman, professor of English Law, offered a swingeing critique of the status of children in our society:

> Children have not been accorded either dignity or respect. They have been reified, denied the status of participants in the social system, labelled as a problem population ... (Freeman, 1987, quoted in Davie, 1993, p. 253)

Indeed, there is a legacy of public perceptions of childhood that has made it difficult, until recently, for people to take seriously the idea of encouraging young people to contribute to debates about things that affect them, both in and out of school.

Austin *et al.* (2003, p. 8) offer comparative evidence of childhood as a culturally specific construction and not a universal 'state', and M. D. A. Freeman (1983, p. 8) reminds us that in England childhood only really became a distinct period around about the seventeenth century and that it was invented by the upper classes 'who alone had the time and money' to support it; later the trend 'diffused downwards through society' (Prout and James, 1997, p. 17). Earlier, young people looked like miniature adults – 'once out of swaddling clothes they adopted the dress of their parents' (M. D. A. Freeman, 1983, p. 8).

There were two dominant images of childhood. One emphasized the natural wildness of children, the other, their natural innocence. An extreme view is expressed by a member of the Wesley family: 'The bias of nature is set the wrong way: education is designed to set it right'; the advice for dealing with these young self-willed creatures was unflinchingly stern: 'Break their wills betimes, begin this work before they can run alone, before they can speak plain, perhaps before they can speak at all. Whatever pains it costs, break the will if you would not damn the child' (in Darling, 1994, pp. 8–9, quoting Southey, 1820). And, of course, the impulse behind mass education was, as Jones (1990, pp. 57–8) has pointed out, a concern 'to regulate the nomadic, dissolute, degenerate, and marginal population of the urban slum'. Teaching was a technology for transforming 'wild beings' into 'ethical subjects'.

The romantic view was equally constraining: the child came from God, 'trailing clouds of glory', entitled to freedom and happiness. Rousseau explored this alternative view of childhood in a treatise, *Emile*, published in 1762, which had, apparently, an electrifying effect: 'Women particularly adored it. Such was the demand that booksellers found it less profitable to sell the book than to rent out copies by the hour' (Darling, 1994, p. 6). In the nineteenth century, public images of childhood which combined innocence and compliance were the stock-in-trade of studio photographers although the stereotyping was to some extent attributable to the long exposure time: children were sometimes given doses of laudanum, a tincture of opium, to ensure that they remained virtuously still. Again and again the same battle was played out – a battle between freedom and control and in relation to young people's bodies and their minds.

The most enduringly comfortable assumption, and one that has shaped policy and practice in many aspects of life, has been that childhood is about dependency. Children are widely thought of as 'incomplete, vulnerable beings progressing with adult help through stages needed to turn them into mature adults' (Mayall, 1994, p. 3); we are preoccupied, says Oakley (1994, p. 23), with their 'becoming' – 'their status as "would-be" adults' – rather than with the here and now state of 'being'; this perception has led us to underestimate their present capabilities. Recent work in the sociology of childhood is an important counterweight to such attitudes and presents an image of young people as accomplished social actors in their own world (James and Prout, 1997, p. ix). In schools, however, it is acknowledged that most young people still lack the power to influence the quality of their lives. It is time to review our notions of childhood.

MacBeath *et al.* remind us of the need to 'get real' about the mix in young people of social maturity, street wisdom and naivety: 'In July 1999 three English teenagers were sent to jail for intimidation, extortion and drug dealing. They had built an extensive network of debtors – children and young people of their own age – trapped into becoming pushers to pay off their escalating debts to the gang, too afraid to tell their parents, too scared to alert the police, not so much because of the consequences of the law as because of the retribution they might face from their terrorist peers' (2000, p. 82).

A few years back, the involvement of two young boys in the death of Jamie Bulger challenged our assumptions about the innocence of childhood and brought a potential for violence into the foreground – even as, earlier, Nabokov's portrayal in *Lolita* of the sexual power and vulnerability of children caused an outcry.

The ambiguities of the child–adult are discussed in the commentary offered by Tiemann on the work which won the John Kobal Photographic Portrait Award of 1999. The photo was of his niece: 'She is 5 and she looks like she could be 12 ... The image is intended to confront the viewer ... You're looking at a child but you're not seeing ideal childhood ... this picture captures an in-between moment between childhood and adulthood' (National Portrait Gallery Exhibition Guide, 1999). This duality is not new but we often choose to see and acknowledge only one side of it.

Outside school, as we have seen above, 'the conception of children as ... inadequately socialized future adults' has been strongly upheld and, as James and Prout (1997, p. xiv) argue, 'it still retains a powerful hold on the social, political, cultural and economic agenda' and explains the kind of selective visibility of young people that Morrow writes about. Her evidence comes from surveys of domestic labour where 'children [are rarely mentioned] as sources of assistance in their homes ... except to a minimal extent in the literature on [girls'] socialisation where such work is seen entirely as role rehearsal for future adulthood and not intrinsically useful or valuable in any way' (Morrow, 1994, p. 134). James and Prout (1997, p. xv) offer further evidence: they mention six problems concerning the visibility of children which were highlighted in a document presented to the UN World Summit on Social Development (1995) by the Save the Children Fund (not all of these of course hold for education, where 'invisibility' is manifest in different ways):

- a failure to collect child-specific information;
- lack of recognition of children's productive contribution;
- no participation of children in decision-making;
- the use of an inappropriate 'standard model of childhood';
- the pursuit of adult interests in ways which render children passive; and
- lack of attention to gender and generational relationships.

In education young people are also vulnerable to an uneasy invisibility. To a teacher trying to manage the restless energy of young people, their noisy high spirits and their attention-seeking behaviours, the idea of 'invisible children' will seem odd. But teachers will recognize the pupils referred to as RHINOS – who are Really Here In Name Only and who have perfected the art of doing relatively little work and at the same time keeping a low profile. But these are not the pupils we are concerned with here. What we are talking about instead is the way that children as a social group have tended to be overlooked in some socio-political settings, and their capacities for autonomous and responsible behaviour underestimated.

Young people's increased status and visibility is apparent in the various labels that we now tie on them in an effort to understand how they are different:

> Today's children and youth have variously been called the Supermarket Generation, the Screen Generation, the Computer Generation; the Nintendo Generation, Techno-kids and Cyberkids. However, other labels such as the Lost Generation, Generation X and Generation Y move beyond such technological reductionism by pointing to wider sources of identity. (Kenway and Bullen, 2001, pp. 55–6)

Generation Y is the first 'to have experienced, from their infancy ... the "computerization of society" and, thus, the effects of hyper reality' (*ibid.*, pp. 16–17). The authors add, citing Nucifora (2000), that 'this is also a generation with heretofore unheard of access to consumer information. Couple that with expanded choice and what results is greater individuality and self-expression' (*ibid.*, p. 57). Young people have emerged as having a significant niche in the market and are consequently courted as consumers. 'Cool', say the authors, 'is an object of desire which can be bought' (p. 48) and they discuss the strategies through which advertisers appeal to young people. A key appeal, interestingly, is the promise of feeling in control and it takes many different forms: young people are offered the possibility of acquiring new skills (such as computer skills), of having their desires met (like wanting to be seen to be older), of being socially acceptable, and of owning things that are socially valued (including mobile phones). Other strategies rely for their appeal on 'contemporary relevance and the "now" factor' (p. 47). Although we may readily recognize the strength of these appeals in relation to adolescents in our families or in our classes in school, we should not delude ourselves by thinking that younger children are not also susceptible.

But the involvement of young people in decision-making affecting their identities and lives is not just about consumerism. Many today are aware that their generation may well have to face a deepening crisis in employment, a growing gap between rich and poor, and an intensification of environmental hazards. Newspapers and TV programmes highlight issues of health (in the wake of fast-food throw-away habits that are encouraging new strains of disease-carrying rodents), of child-bearing (as familiar boundaries dissolve in the context of surrogate mothering), of everyday eating (as the risks and benefits of genetically modified food continue to be debated). All these issues are prominent in decision-making arenas that may well affect the lives of young people currently in school and we have to ask whether the agenda that is prioritized in schools is equipping them to cope – to weigh evidence, to take account of different perspectives on an issue, to develop a position on an issue and to be prepared to modify it in the light of new evidence. The introduction of citizenship education in the national curriculum may provide a framework for helping young people to explore such issues.

Kenway and Bullen summarize Australian teachers' comments on how difficult the young people they teach today are:

> They are often considered more troublesome than students of former decades. They are more easily bored, restless and hard to control. They are also less attentive and respectful, and far less interested in their school word. Many seem to come grudgingly to school. They are apathetic and disengaged when in class, 'turn on' mainly with their peers and seem to get their pleasures, find their identities and, indeed, live the 'important' parts of their lives elsewhere – out of class, out of school. (Kenway and Bullen, 2001, p. 1)

This may be an overstatement. Nonetheless it is important for us to understand what the out-of-school world of young people is like and what learning in school looks like from their perspective. We cannot – and should not want to – keep the world outside school away from the world inside school, and that means changing our perceptions not only of the young people we teach but also of the assumptions that keep traditional structures and relationships in place.

A closer look at schools

Our argument here is that despite wave after wave of curriculum reform, schools have not changed as much as we might have expected. It is echoed by Lawton (2001, p. 1) who said, '... schools have been slower to change than other institutions such as factories. In many respects schools are now out of step with the rest of society'. Hirsch, narrowing the focus to the middle years of schooling and the content of the curriculum, draws atention to the difficulties that transfer presents for young people at a complex stage in their lives:

> In many countries [this is] a time when a number of new pressures and requirements arise simultaneously. Not only must the student get used to the increased rigors of secondary school, but the curriculum is generally fuller than at any other stage. Foreign languages, particular social and natural science disciplines, and subjects such as technology and computer studies get added to the curriculum ... At the same time, there is an evident need to raise the awareness of the young adolescent in less academic areas such as health, citizenship, and sex education. The pressures ... are crowding in from every angle. (Hirsch, 1998, p. 75)

Holloway and Valentine, more recently still, take a similar line:

> Children spend most of the weekday in a very time-disciplined environ-ment at school where all their activities from arrival, registration and lessons, through to eating and playing, are governed by the daily rhythm of timetables and bells which signal the choreographed mass movements of pupils within the school. (Holloway and Valentine, 2003, p. 108)

Many decades earlier, Harold Dent, historian, editor of the *Times Educational Supplement* and former headteacher, also criticized the lack of time/space for young people in school: 'The first characteristic of the secondary school boy [*sic*], to my mind, is his intense vitality [but] his vitality must express itself in action' and in school 'he has not a moment to spare; his whole day is occupied, and with school affairs' (Dent, 1927, pp. 209, 211). Dent's strategy was to create space. In an article published 12 years later he describes how, as headteacher of a boys' school, he did this, and with what impact:

> I gave instructions that each pupil was to have a certain number of periods during the week in which he was free to do exactly what he pleased, short of creating such a disturbance as would interrupt the work of others. Various rooms were equipped with materials for drawing, painting, wood-working, model engineering, and scissors-and-paste hobbies, and a library and reading-room was available. But it was clearly understood that pupils were not restricted to these special rooms if they found interests elsewhere … This period of observation lasted for a whole term. What were the results? From the point of view of formal instruction in academic subjects they were in many cases disastrous. But with few exceptions they made progress along other lines which was literally amazing. For example, two older boys, aged about fifteen, wired for electric light the cellars beneath the school and a number of unoccupied rooms … Another group spent practically all its time in the local museum compiling a history of the city … Many of the boys were utterly different creatures by the end of the term; they had developed poise, self-confidence and skill, and there was little difficulty in fitting them into courses which were calculated to give them present satisfaction and a sure basis for the future. (Dent, 1939, pp. 391, 392)

This experience enabled Dent to offer a broader principle for the structuring of pupils' experiences in secondary school; he suggested that young adolescents should have a year out from the usual pressures of a structured curriculum in order to find and explore new interests and talents:

> I would make the bolder suggestion that, after the two-year period of general education, from eleven to thirteen, there should follow a period of twelve months during which formal instruction, and indeed formal courses of any kind, are cut to the minimum, and pupils are left largely to their own devices, in an environment calculated to develop the creative and inquisitive instincts, so that both inclinations and aptitudes may demonstrate themselves, and a wise and permanent choice may be made for the … years which remain of the secondary school course. (Dent, 1939, p. 393)

How wastefully subversive this sounds to us today in the present climate of pressurized activity but the concern that prompted this approach is one that we should be sympathetic to – it is about ensuring that *all* pupils are supported in school in discovering their aptitudes and working at the far edges of their potential.

In England, the foundations of our system of state schooling did not favour the development of the idea of 'education for all'; the system was designed to have a particular impact on a particular segment of the population, as Lawton (2001) makes clear:

> The school as we know it now was largely a 19th century invention deriving from 19th century social theories and practices which gave rise to a number of different kinds of institutions such as workhouses, factories and prisons. Schools shared a number of their characteristics – including architecture. Such institutions were developed to solve social and economic problems. What they had in common was the need for a large number of 'inmates' to be *controlled* by a smaller number of supervisors. In all cases there were two features in common: strict discipline and hard labour. And to make the task of the supervisors possible certain practices and rules became customary, for example, silence, strict control over time (marked by bells, sirens or hooters) and restrictions of space (sitting in rows ...) and movement (such as marching in lock-step). Many rules were necessary for this bureaucratic-autocratic form of organisation. In all cases, including schools, *control* was the dominant factor. (Lawton, 2001, p. 1)

Similar pictures of control and moral colonialism are painted by other historians and social theorists: 'As nineteenth-century philanthropy identified the undifferentiated squalor of the city as an object of concern, it introduced a pedagogical machinery to normalize it', says Jones (1990, p. 57–8). And Boren (2001, p. 27) comments on the charity schools of the eighteenth century: 'These institutions were not simply philanthropic endeavours but a means of social control meant to foster a prescribed morality, a respect for the existing social order, and social discipline – instigated by the wealthy, who feared the lower classes and social unrest.'

State schooling has bound into its structures a thick set of class-based assumptions about power and control which are manifest in a legacy of 'dividing practices' (Meadmore, 1993); they are deep-rooted and difficult to eradicate because they are part of the taken-for-grantedness of institutional life. We would argue that their pervasiveness makes it fundamentally difficult to enact democratic practices in the everyday life of our schools. And yet, despite the hegemony of performance-thinking, which subtly reinforces these dividing practices, in some schools issues of community, consultation and participation are firmly on the agenda.

Our evidence suggests that a stronger focus on pupil participation (we see consultation as a form of participation) can enhance progress in learning. The greater involvement of pupils is not therefore necessarily in opposition to the government's standards agenda – and it explicitly feeds into the new citizenship agenda.

Jamieson and Wikeley suggest that 'schools need to systematically find out as much as they can about the interests and concerns of their young people and use this information as a starting point to debate and work with young people in designing the arrangements of schooling' (2000, p. 446). And they make the point that the kind of professional flexibility and autonomy that is good for pupils is also good for teachers: 'Just as students are unlikely to be motivated to work hard if they see that they have to conform to an unyielding model of work tasks and school organisation, so teachers are unlikely to give of their best if they are presented with a teacher-proofed model of teaching' (*ibid.*).

Seymour, writing in the context of involving pupils as stakeholders in the design of new schools, makes a similar point: 'In the world beyond the school gates, students are surrounded by modern technology that enables them to access the images, sounds and text that interest them, *at their own pace*. The workplace is also changing. Management structures are flatter, working arrangements are more flexible, and there is a greater emphasis on team work' (Seymour *et al.*, 2001, p. 15; emphasis added). If new assumptions about the status of pupils and the ways in which people work best can be reflected in the spaces of new schools then the kind of changes that seem to us to be important may more easily follow. Sadly, the reality is that most pupils will continue to be educated in buildings where the messages of the architecture need actively to be neutralized.

The *Guardian* published a survey in 2001 (an update on Blishen's 1969 exercise) on 'How I'd Like Schools To Be'. It's impossible to know, in prize-winning events, how independently students wrote their contributions but the outcomes are still interesting. Fifteen thousand students aged five to 18 responded and the top five ideas included 'being listened to':

- *Beautiful schools* – full of light, airy, with uncluttered class-rooms and brightly coloured walls.
- *Comfortable schools* – with sofas, beanbags, blinds that keep the sun out, and with quiet rooms where you can sometimes be on your own and think.
- *Safe schools* – with swipe cards, anti-bully alarms, places you can go to if you are sick, lockers that are *yours*, and people to talk over problems with.
- *Listening schools* – with lots of discussion between students and teachers, and the chance to talk to governors and help choose teachers – you'd work harder for teachers if you knew that your mates had chosen them.
- *Flexible schools* – where you have time to finish things you are interested in instead of stopping when the bell goes, where you can do lots of projects and work on real-life problems.

There were some intriguing individual ideas. One student wanted a school where butterflies fly under a glass roof, another wanted (without explaining why, or what it was!) a Wild Child Centre; some comments were very modest and down to earth – clean toilets, sharp pencils, someone to fill in the holes in the tarmac in the playground, and teachers who always tell you *why* you are learning something.

Those who are sceptical about making schools places where young people are encouraged to think for themselves, to play a part in institutional decision-making and to be encouraged to express their views may well be anxious lest such 'freedoms' will lead to 'trouble'. Indeed, critics may well remember that in the early nineteenth century there was a national wave of children's strikes. Among them was the Burston School Strike in Norfolk (which lasted from 1914 to 1917) where the pupils' action was not so much a protest about the general conditions of schooling but an expression of solidarity and support for two teachers who had been dismissed (see Edwards, 1974). The student power movements of the 1960s and 1970s (see the National Union of School Students (NUSS) declaration on page 108) were more directly about the right to participate but they were more prominent in higher education where, according to Ben Levin

(1999), 'a student presence in governance and student evaluations of teaching' have become standard university practice. In schools, he goes on, although a minority sit on staff appointments panels, pupils are not, at the moment, much concerned with matters of governance although this will change as citizenship education develops. They are, however, being encouraged to shape the conditions of learning in lessons and they are concerned about being treated fairly and with reasonable respect:

> Students ... want to have something to say about how they learn, when they learn, where they learn, and so on. Many matters that have traditionally been assumed to be the purview of the teachers will become instead matters to be discussed and negotiated with students.

And Levin ends his paper with a line that will also serve as a final statement in this chapter: 'This kind of discussion is critical to learning.'

2 Don't Underestimate Pupils

As a result of stories in the media, and our own observations, we are increasingly aware of the differences between the roles and responsibilities pupils have out of school and those they have in school. A 15-year-old young woman in a single-parent family talks about the domestic chores she has in the evenings – which leave her little time or energy for her homework: 'It's come in, put the washing on, get the dinner ready, get the kids in, then my dad comes in and its dinner in the oven, washing up – it's housework I do, not homework' (Rudduck, 1999, p. 46). Another 15-year-old young woman, described in school as surly and difficult, out of school is a lively, gutsy singer (as we heard on a recording!) and, accompanied by her father, entertains in the working men's clubs in the north of England. A 17-year-old boy, slightly gauche in school when talking to his teachers, is transformed when he walks onto the concert platform as the young pianist invited by a music group to play with them in a quintet. And a 15-year-old girl, rather inactive and nondescript in school, at the weekend assumes a professional identity, style and degree of poise as a hairdresser's assistant.

More unusual and high profile evidence of young people's capabilities is presented in the account of *The Learning School* project (MacBeath and Sugimine, 2003). Three successive groups of young people aged between 16 and 18 spent 12 months visiting and evaluating secondary schools in the eight participating countries: the Czech Republic, Germany, Hong Kong, Korea, Japan, Scotland, South Africa and Sweden. After being trained in basic research methods they spent up to six weeks looking at each of the eight secondary schools, one from each country. They had to learn what being part of a team meant and how to get on with the diversity of people they met – not only within the team but also in the schools they studied and in the families they stayed with. Learning to understand and respect different cultures and be aware of their own cultural assumptions was also a major challenge. They were accompanied for the year by two student co-ordinators and by a teacher. What they achieved, intellectually, socially and personally, was remarkable.

There were clearly many problems to be confronted and worked through – being away from home, travelling, speaking in English, meeting real deadlines and dealing with irritations and frustrations generated by other members of the team without losing the team spirit. And, compared with their lives in school, they also had to cope with a disorienting lack of structure which may or may not have been deliberate but which, retrospectively, they rated positively:

> I'm glad there wasn't much prepared for us. Before I almost cursed it but now I praise it instead. Inexperienced as we were, guidelines would have been very useful but there was almost none. So it was up to us to make the best of the year and I feel that we did. The feeling of achievement is now greater because it was up to us that accomplished it. With some help from the universities and the schools, the end result is above my first expectations. (Jimmy, p. 37)

Students reflected on their own growth:

> Before I joined Learning School, motivation was something I never thought of and suddenly I had to find out what made other students want to learn, before I knew what made me learn. (Karolina, p. 10)

> Gradually I learned not to see things just from my view and to try to think from different aspects . . . It was also at the same time that I started to doubt what I took for granted. (Kazuyo, p. 37)

> [What I learnt] is that sometimes you have to adapt to certain situations in order to keep the peace. Sometimes saying nothing is the best way of saying something. (Jolene, p. 42)

The comments of some 'expert witnesses' are included in the book. They write largely on the basis of having seen the students present their experiences and findings at the end of their year – and before they re-joined their schools. They were seen as articulate, poised and socially mature. So impressive were they that a former Scottish Chief Inspector suggested (see MacBeath and Sugimine 2003, p. 67) that pupils might in future be included in inspection teams. Of course, these young people were working outside the boundaries of formal schooling, but, having demonstrated what they are capable of doing when given the chance, their story might encourage schools to find ways of releasing young people's potential by offering them the right balance of challenge and support in the context of school improvement in their everyday settings.

Indeed, a perennial plea of young people is to be given more responsibility and be treated in more adult ways in school. Their expectations are highest as they anticipate the move to 'the big school' but their aspiration appears to elude them most of the time – it is nearly always a promise for the *next* year:

> Y6: It's going to be really exciting, being an adult – well, kind of an adult.
>
> Y7: It toughens you up coming to secondary school. At primary school you sort of become soft.
>
> Y8: Now we're Year 8s, we don't get treated like we did last year. We get looked at more maturely by the teachers. And also the first years look up to us as well – that's quite nice! . . . Teachers trust you a bit more. Like in Science you didn't do anything with chemicals but now you do like dangerous experiments.
>
> Y9: The one thing I hate about school is being treated like a three-year-old. I want to feel like an adult.
>
> Y10: Work experience made me look at my future and it were a lot different to school. They treated me like an adult and it were good. It were really good the way they treated me.
>
> Y11: I feel more adult in Year 11 with us being the oldest and looking down at the others. And then one of the teachers will come along and you like look up at them and think, 'No. I'm not an adult yet!' (Rudduck, Wallace and Day, 2000, p. 24)

It is important to find ways of acknowledging young people's sense of increasing maturity and status as they move through the years of primary and secondary school but the right mix of task and trust is not always there. Of course it can be argued that taking on additional roles can get in the way of pupils' main responsibility, which is to learn, but our counter argument is that young people today are more likely to commit themselves to learning in organizations that recognize their capabilities. Moreover, the broader learnings acquired by *The Learning School* team of students but not usually reflected in exam grades are ones that will serve young people – and society – well in their lives beyond school.

What kinds of roles and responsibilities *are* widely available to young people in schools today? Evidence from a range of school studies suggests that the traditional and limited 'regulatory' roles – such as monitors or prefects – are giving way to a broader range of 'social/institutional' and 'pedagogic' roles. As pupils' capability is recognized, so the range increases. In the next section we present some examples. We do not claim that these are new roles – some schools have long had a culture in which young people participate fully in the life and work of their school. All we are saying is that more schools today seem to be interested in finding different ways in which young people can feel responsible, feel that they are contributing and feel that they belong. These initiatives will undoubtedly grow in the wake of the citizenship agenda in schools.

Examples of regulatory roles

The most familiar 'regulatory' role in the past has been that of prefect or monitor: pupils were an extension of the surveillance structures of the school and were given additional status relative to their peers to help keep order in the school, particularly in the breaks between lessons. The roles were often marked by 'badges of office' (such as prefect shields) and there might be privileges, such as a prefects' common room which imitated in some way the staff common room. Ball writes about the regulatory work in schools in terms of an 'observing hierarchy' (1990, p. 159) – whose ranks those pupils in prefect roles are invited to join. But some 'softer' regulatory roles are now being introduced in schools – for instance, the 'mediator' role.

The 'mediator' role

Concern with harassment and bullying has led a number of schools to look at ways of involving students in finding solutions to social problems. Indeed, Wyness (2000, p. 108) argues that children possess many mediation skills and that they are 'better equipped than adults to deal with conflict between pupils for the simple reason that they are more knowledgeable about what goes on in the playground'. Students in both primary and secondary schools have been carefully briefed to take the role of anti-bullying counsellors, providing support to those who are being bullied and helping to resolve difficult situations outside the classroom. A primary school we worked with introduced what they called 'the mediator project' (see Doddington *et al.*, 1999, p. 13); the success of the scheme is communicated by teachers' stories, including one about an incident in which a Year 3 mediator (a girl) single-handedly resolved an acrimonious football dispute among Year 6 boys. The Year 3 pupil showed a remarkable level of maturity and skill in liaising with the boys over three lunchtimes before finally reaching a successful conclusion. A period of training gives self-confidence and a professional edge to such work.

Collaborative problem-solving

The second example is of a collaborative effort to solve the problem of classroom noise. Teachers at another primary school were concerned about pupils who seemed disengaged. They asked them to talk about what helped them to learn and what got in the way of their learning. They found that pupils could readily identify things that affected their concentration and prevented them from doing their best. One of the things most frequently mentioned as problematic was noise in the classroom. The headteacher followed up the enquiry by inviting pupils from each year group to work with him on solving the problem and they came up with a colour-coded 'voice system'. It described the voice levels pupils and teachers thought were suitable for different occasions and different settings:

Silence (pale blue)

We talk only if we really have to so that we don't disturb other people and we put our hands up when we want to talk to the teacher.

Partner voice (royal blue)

Only the person we are talking to can hear what we are saying.

Table voice (green)

One person speaks at a time whilst everyone else on the table listens but only people on our table should be able to hear us.

Class voice (yellow)

One person in the class speaks at a time but loudly enough for everyone to be able to hear while everyone else listens.

Playground voice (red)

We can use this voice to call each other when we are outside.

Copies of the code were printed on cards and posters and put prominently around the school. The fact that this was seen as the pupils' own system meant that they were more likely to persuade their peers to respect it and the colour links seemed to make it easier for pupils to remember the 'rules' (see Flutter *et al.*, 1998).

In a secondary school where about half of one year group didn't do their homework regularly in modern foreign languages, the MFL teacher decided to enlist the help of the group in solving the problem. The outcome was that instead of giving pupils their homework at the end of each lesson, to be done that evening, she gave them a list of all the weekly homeworks which they had to do over a term. This list was written in the target language for the pupils but with a copy in English which went back to the parents. The critical element in the scheme was the appointment of a series of pupil monitors whose job it was to check, at the end of each week, which homeworks had been done and by which children. The outcome was that the completion rates for homework went up from 50 per cent to over 80 per cent. The pupils said that they were much happier because they could do their homeworks at a time during the week which suited them and they felt less 'hunted' by the pupil monitor than by the teacher. It seems that the regulatory role of the monitors was softened by their being 'elected' by their peers: every week the pupil whose homework was judged by the others to be the best was given a special certificate and became the next week's monitor (Barry Jones's field work data).

Examples of social/institutional roles

It is not uncommon for pupils to act as guides to visitors who want to see round the school, to work at reception on open days, to sell produce at stalls during breaks, to act as stage managers for school productions, to act as spokesperson for their class at year or school council meetings. Criticisms can be levelled at such practices on the grounds that if they happen during the school day then they take pupils away from lessons. But if there are clear procedures for catching up then the trust invested in pupils through these roles can enhance their self-esteem and their sense of being part of the school community and this in turn can strengthen their commitment to learning. More recently we have come across some other ways in which schools offer young people a chance to participate in and contribute to the school's affairs.

Interviewing staff applicants

The idea of involving pupils in selecting applicants for both teaching and non-teaching posts has been tried by a number of primary and secondary schools and has been common practice in some education systems for decades. At one secondary school a student panel interviews applicants for teaching posts in addition to the usual panel of governors, teachers and others. Candidates interviewed said they were impressed with the serious and insightful way in which students questioned prospective teachers. At another secondary school, applicants for a teaching post are asked to give a trial lesson which the pupils involved evaluate; at some point each applicant meets pupils on one of the school council subcommittees for a short interview. As the senior management team explain, if applicants think this is an odd way to proceed then they are not right for a school in which pupil voice is an important feature.

Of course, these strategies are not without their regulatory dimension: there is some expectation that if pupils are involved in appointing new teachers they will feel some responsibility towards them and will be less inclined to mess about in their lessons. However, this argument assumes that pupils beyond those who were involved in the interviews also feel a sense of responsibility – and indeed this *can* be achieved but only by inviting a larger number of pupils to discuss and report on the qualities needed for a particular position and the questions that might be asked of applicants.

One successful teacher described how being interviewed by students gave her an immediate appreciation of the value the school placed on student consultation and participation and of the way in which it strengthened the rapport between staff and students. At another secondary school students take an active part in interviewing non-teaching staff; students see the point of being given an opportunity to choose meals supervisors, caretakers and learning support assistants.

Helping sustain a good learning environment

In some schools students are given responsibility for various aspects of the school environment – not just keeping their designated social area clean but rather more creative tasks, such as designing and maintaining a conservation area; designing and making murals for corridors; or designing and fitting out student common rooms. At a local primary school students were consulted about their school environment (see Flutter *et al.*, 1998) and their comments about colour, lighting and seating were taken into consideration in a subsequent improvement programme in the school. And teachers at an infants school were surprised at the astuteness of the comments of Reception and Year 1 students on their school environment; one outcome of the enquiry was a decision that the student body should be involved in discussions with architects about the design of their new school. At a primary school pupils were invited to contribute to the planning of their new play area – and, according to the then deputy head, Alison Peacock, offered some ideas that teachers would not have thought of: the pupils wanted a wildlife patch, a corner where you could 'just dig', a 'sad area' which was more private and where you could go if you felt miserable, a low stage for plays and performances and a fountain.

At a secondary school the headteacher, as part of the school's provision for citizenship education, introduced a form of Prime Minister's Question Time for the older forms – with the headteacher receiving and having to respond to the questions put to her. She noted that a number of questions were about the school environment, including these:

> What can be done to relieve congestion in the corridors?
>
> We have been told in our science lessons that we should drink a pint of water a day. Why then are the water fountains not working?

The assistant head commented that such events, which were part of a broader plan to encourage consultation and participation, helped 'foster a genuine sense of pupil ownership of the school'; she was also struck by the good sense of the questions and was concerned that the school had, in the past, been underestimating both pupils' concern about the quality of the school environment and their capacity for identifying and presenting real issues in a constructive way (see Negrine, 2002, p. 4). The plan is to extend the event to younger pupils in the school.

Concerns about the corridors also surface in the 2001 publication, *School Works Toolkit*. The initiative was sponsored by the Paul Hamlyn Foundation and the Construction Industry Training Board and it aimed to explore designs that work, that are aesthetically exciting and at the same time support learning. Importantly, consultation with key stakeholders – including pupils – is an important aspect of the process: 'School Works is all about participation: it involves the people who learn and work everyday in your school in the decisions that will affect the school building and its design maintenance.' The voices of the users are there from the beginning of any initiative:

> The initial ideas are generated by the school community being asked for their reactions to a preconceived design agenda ... It is a democratic approach that will give the project credibility amongst users and the wider community. (2001, p. 11)

The cycles of debate, exploration of issues and consensus building are repeated at different stages of the project. In one school corridors were mentioned a lot by pupils and teachers as a site of harassment and anxiety. Because a widening of the corridors was not really possible, the design team set up discussions among users; these intensive in-context reviews led, for example, to the possibility that the problem was not so much with the original width of the corridor but with the organization of the school day and the fact that everyone in the school changed classes at the same time. Another problem often identified by pupils is the lack of personal space – including lockers. Focus group discussion among pupils in another school revealed that this not only affected young people's sense of belonging but also their learning in that they were reluctant to bring all they needed to school because it was a lot to carry round all day. The consultation started with pupils listing and commenting on what they carried around with them on a typical day; they were then invited to suggest and review different ways of solving the problem. Issues of territory and sense of community were raised as well as questions of security (pp. 41, 86). Solutions were arrived at that were colourful, manageable, that met the concerns of teachers, parents and pupils – and that those involved felt were 'theirs'.

Examples of pedagogic roles

MacBeath and Sugimine (2003, p. 1), commenting on the achievements of their team of young researchers from schools across the world, suggest that their experience 'gives the lie to the recent words of the [English] ex-Chief Inspector of Schools who wrote: "Teachers teach and children learn. It is as simple as that" (Woodhead, 2002)'. In fact, we often encounter young people who are successfully teaching each other and learning from each other. The most common structure, in both primary and secondary schools, is peer tutoring.

Peer tutoring schemes have been a regular practice in some schools since the 1980s (see Topping, 1988; Goodlad, 1998). They involve a commitment to giving young people responsibilities that have traditionally resided exclusively with the teacher. Many young people in primary and secondary schools are now involved in some form of tutoring in their own or in another school. Year 9s may have spent time with Year 7 pupils helping them to find their way around the school; Year 11s may spend some time each week with Year 8 pupils, helping them with reading; or Year 8s may visit Year 6 pupils in the primary school to answer questions about their imminent move to 'the big school'; or pupils from the junior school may work with infants to help them with their reading and writing. Of course, many schools have traditionally had prefect systems where older pupils have a *control* responsibility in relation to other pupils but, as a result of these various tutoring initiatives, we are now beginning to recognize the contribution that pupils can formally make to each other's learning: they are moving from a control to a support framework.

An obvious characteristic of tutor pairings is that there is invariably an asymmetry of relationship, with the mentor's position premised on some superiority, whether of knowledge or skill or age. The focus may be informative, as when older pupils answer younger pupils' questions about procedures and protocols; it may be social/regulatory (as we saw earlier in this section) when pupils take on mediator roles in situations where there are peer disputes; or it may be pedagogic, as when pupils are trying to support the learning of their peers. The pedagogic role seems to have been fairly widely developed in relation to basic skills such as reading and computation. Procedurally, the weight of the evidence suggests that in cross-age partnerships the optimum age gap is two or three years, that the competence gap should not be too extreme and that most pupils prefer same-sex pairings (see Morrison *et al.*, 2000, p. 189). Moreover, the evidence suggests (see Shanahan, 1998) that the self-esteem of both tutor and tutee can be enhanced as a consequence of their involvement in the process and that gains are not limited to the academic basis of the partnership.

Morrison *et al.* (2000) report a study of peer-tutoring in a primary and secondary school. The schools were interesting for several reasons: neither had had previous experience of the potential of peer tutoring; both were interested in social and attitudinal outcomes as well as academic; in both, the academic concern was with literacy skills. In the primary school, four-year-old pupils were supported by eight-year-old pupils; in the secondary school, Year 7 pupils were supported by Year 9 pupils. In the primary school the academic focus was on extending pupils' meaningful use, in reading and writing, of an individualized set of words which the child found difficult; in the secondary school the focus was on the attitudes to reading and reading skills of a group of lower-achieving boys.

In the primary school five pairs of pupils tried out the approach; five pupils who needed to improve their vocabulary were identified from the Reception class and they were paired with volunteers from Year 4. The older pupils, after the teacher had fully explained what the tutoring involved, 'applied' to be a partner. Here are some extracts from the application forms:

I think I will be able to give my partner quite a lot of help. I think I will particularly be able to help them decide on what they want to write about by speaking to them.

I will help them improve their skill at reading so your class will start likeing more stories. Soon they will be nice and smart for you.

I could help them to read some bigger words and I would tell them what the words mean so they would understand them later in there school years. (Morrison *et al.*, 2000, pp. 197–8; original spelling)

There was one girl–girl pair, three girl–boy pairs and one boy–girl pair (the older pupil being listed first). The framework for the paired work was the production of a booklet that told a story and the work was completed in two sessions. First, the older children asked their partners abut the story that they wanted to write; the younger child then drew pictures of the key moments while their partner wrote the story down, making sure that the 'target words' provided by the teacher for that pupil were included. Two versions of the story were then produced, one long and illustrated and the other short, in large print and highlighting the key words for the younger child to practise reading. The longer versions were typed by a teacher and made into booklets.

Not surprisingly, in the short time available for the lessons, there was no evidence of improvements in the younger children's reading or in sight vocabulary. However, there was evidence from the follow-up interviews that younger and older pupils held more positive feelings about reading and writing, particularly as a result of seeing how good the story booklets looked when they were finished. Socially there were noticeable benefits in that the pairs looked out for each other outside the classroom at break times (there is often an aspiration that the cross-age tutoring will help to minimize the bullying of younger pupils by older pupils).

The secondary school also chose to have older pupils helping younger pupils with their reading and, in the context of national concern about boys' performance, the school decided to restrict the research to boys. Ten Year 7 boys, whose average reading age was 8.5, were selected and they were divided into two groups. One group was paired with five competent Year 9 readers and the other with five less competent Year 9 readers. The pairs met twice weekly for 30 minutes at the start of the day over a 10-week period. An interesting additional dimension to the project was the fact that the Year 9 boys were selected from two very different social groupings. The five competent readers were confident, were held in high esteem within the school and were successful academically. The other five Year 9 boys had struggled academically and their behaviour had been problematic from time to time. This second group had experienced difficulties within their peer group – either as bully or as victim – and their self-esteem was generally poor. It was hoped that by being selected as tutors their self-esteem might be raised. The older boys did not know the basis on which they had been selected: one *good reader* said, 'I think I was chosen to take part in the project because I am reliable' and another said that he was doing this for 'the satisfaction that I have helped someone to do better with their life'; a *poor reader* said that he had been chosen 'because I can listen to children and it would kind of help me in my reading' and another said that he wanted to be involved 'hopefully (to get) a "thank you"'.

The reading skills of the Year 7 and Year 9 boys were tested using a group reading test. There was a training session for the Year 9 boys, run by the school's Special Needs Co-ordinator, to enable them to deal sensitively with their Year 7 partners. At the end of the project all the pupils involved were retested for reading skills and were interviewed by a researcher about their experiences and their views of the project. Overall, the reading levels, as measured by the testing, were not significantly raised but there was clear evidence of enhanced motivation to read. Indeed, the attitude of all participants at the end of the project was extremely positive:

> I am reading more books now, and more difficult books. (Y7)
>
> I read with my mum at home now. (Y7: this pupil's mother wrote a letter to the school thanking them for 'inspiring him to read'.)
>
> It was brilliant – great fun! (Y7)
>
> I read with my younger brother now. (Y9)
>
> We gained friendship. (Y9)

In another secondary school in a different LEA we worked with a high-achieving school in developing peer mentoring with a more general focus. The project compared Year 8 pupils' experiences of being tutored by Year 12s and by teachers. The purpose of the tutor meetings was to provide opportunities for Year 8 pupils to discuss progress, to highlight their achievements and to share problems with a more experienced learner, whether older student or teacher. Overt note-taking did not take place during the mentor meeting and no written records were kept of the sessions (see Batty *et al.*, 1999, pp. 368–9).

All the mentors – staff and the students – received training that concentrated on interpersonal process skills:

- appropriate ways of opening a session;
- keeping the discussion going, encouraging reflection;
- closing the mentoring session;
- open questioning techniques that would allow students to do most of the talking.

The guidelines for mentors included the following statements (this is not a comprehensive list):

- try not to make judgments or provide answers, but instead help students develop coping strategies;
- try not to trivialize what the Year 8 students feel is important;
- try to listen more than talk and avoid silences which Year 8 students might find intimidating;
- try to pick up on the positive aspects and give Year 8 students the opportunity to expand on what they do well;
- try to encourage students to clarify the situation by thinking aloud;
- respect confidentiality (but make it clear that sometimes it may be necessary to pass on information);
- try to listen and accept.

The Year 8 students were given an abridged set of these guidelines. Half were then mentored by Year 12 students and half by teachers.

After the period of mentoring the Year 8s talked about the advantages and disadvantages of having students or teachers as mentors. Teachers' strengths included their skills in handling the discussion and the resources that they can bring to bear on a problem.

The negative aspect of having a teacher as mentor is concern lest they talk about you and your problems to other teachers. There was also some anxiety about the protocol of telling a teacher about the difficulties you have in another teacher's lessons. The strength of the Year 12s is that they are closer in age and experience. However, the Year 8s were also aware of the limitations of sixth formers. They were seen as less reliable than teachers, less 'committed' to the well-being of the Year 8s and likely to talk about their mentees to their friends. Since this issue was also raised in relation to teachers, it indicates the importance of privacy and confidentiality in a system where so much of what young people do in school is recorded or made public.

The pupils were also insightful in discussing the qualities that would make a good mentor. The good mentor needs to be someone who is reliable – as we have already heard – and also someone who:

- is approachable, is a good listener and is interested in what you have to say;
- is trustworthy and will keep your confidences;
- has the skill to encourage you to talk and is not too intrusive or pushy;
- is knowledgeable and experienced;

This statement summed it up:

> [A good mentor is] someone who seems interested in what you're saying even if to them it's not interesting. Your problems might seem really minor to them because they're older and probably they've experienced bigger problems than yours but they have to act as though they're interested in what you are saying. (Y8)

*

This chapter, called *Don't Underestimate Pupils*, has tried to demonstrate not only the different roles that pupils are successfully taking in schools but also their capacity to reflect, analytically and constructively – when given space and encouragement – on aspects of learning that are important to them. The next chapter shows how their insights have made a difference to both policy and practice.

3 Making A Difference

Can what pupils tell us make a difference? Our answer – and that of many teachers we have worked with – is emphatically 'yes'. Pupil commentaries on teaching and learning in school provide a practical agenda for change that can help fine-tune or, more fundamentally, identify and shape improvement strategies. The insights from their world can help us to 'see' things that we do not normally pay attention to but that matter to them.

The purpose of this chapter is to demonstrate the power of pupil commentary, particularly in relation to teaching and learning. In some situations pupils may be explicitly consulted about what affects their learning so that they are knowingly contributing to the process of improvement. In others, their sense of agency and involvement is less obvious as teachers or external researchers interpret what they say in the context of other narratives. While the former approach is more empowering for pupils, the latter enables listening and responsive adults to see significance in something that they might not otherwise have thought about. For instance, when a pupil happened to say, in passing, 'School's great – apart from the lessons' (Harris *et al.*, 1994), she unwittingly prompted a line of enquiry that led, eventually, to a project reviewing the balance of social and academic activities in induction procedures at transfer.

We have chosen a number of topics to illustrate the extent to which interviews and conversations with pupils have helped us understand the conditions of learning in school. In some cases the content of pupil commentaries echoes powerfully across schools and has been widely acted on (as with the analysis of learning in Year 8). All the examples are from projects that we have been responsible for or involved in (see pages 159–65). They illuminate aspects of:

- the organizational dimension of learning in school;
- the individual dimension;
- the pedagogic dimension of learning in school;
- the social dimension of learning in school.

The Organizational Dimension

By 'organizational dimension of learning' we mean the broad policies that shape and colour, limit and extend pupils' experiences as learners. We have chosen two topics where we have substantial sets of commentaries from pupils across schools and where we think that pupil observations have really made a difference to school policy and even to national policy:

- transfer and learning; and
- the Year 8 and Year 3 'dips' in progress.

In each case we were trying to tease out, from young people's testimony, how different things about the way learning is organized or managed are perceived or experienced by pupils as enabling or getting in the way of their learning.

Transfer and learning

There has been a long tradition in transfer studies of eliciting the perspectives of the pupils themselves – and the accounts they offered have undoubtedly led to change. Earlier research (e.g. Nisbet and Entwistle, 1969; Power and Cotterell, 1981; Murdoch, 1982; Measor and Woods, 1984; Beynon, 1985; Waterhouse, 1992) highlighted the anxiety and bewilderment that pupils felt as they were about to move from the familiar world of the primary school to what Hirsch (1998) called the 'jungle' of the secondary school. Pupils from other countries with a similar transfer arrangement expressed similar concerns; these are the words of a young Finnish student:

> What worries me about the [move] to secondary school is ... whether I will find my way to the right classrooms and how the teachers and classmates will relate to me ... I think at least in my future class I should find many new friends. And I hope that my classmates will

relate to me in a positive way and don't avoid me or discriminate against me ... At primary school I am used to a small class, during these six years. The classes will probably be much bigger at secondary school but I guess one just has to get used to it ... I also expect that teaching will be more difficult at secondary school because the class is much bigger and there will be many more new subjects ... (quoted by Pietarinen, 2000, p. 388)

In the wake of the earlier research, so much attention has been given by teachers to the social well-being of pupils as they confronted and managed the move to the 'big school' that it has become the ultimate user-friendly experience: there are open days before the start of the new school year and taster sessions where pupils are helped to feel good about new and potentially daunting subjects; there are simple practical 'guides' to life in the new school, welcoming social events, off-campus bonding sessions for new groups of pupils, and so on. Ironically, it seems that teachers' attempts to minimize anxiety and make new pupils feel 'at home' are often countered by older pupils' concerns to *enhance* anxiety: their 'welcoming' rituals are designed to make newcomers feel small and know their place in the established hierarchy: Year 7s *are* thrown over walls, rolled down hills, chased round the grounds. And there are other hazards that they might not have anticipated: they get blisters walking round the big site in new shoes; they don't arrive at the right classroom at the right time; they wear the wrong clothes to the first disco: 'We wore jeans and high heels and a nice top and everyone else were in shell suits – it were dead embarrasing' (Harris and Rudduck, 1993, p. 327). At the old school they knew the ropes and they were 'the top'; now they are the most vulnerable, as a Norwegian researcher explains: 'Seen through the eyes of the pupils, it is not just a great transition, but also a great fall – in the feeling of social mastery, status, power, and security – that occurs almost overnight' (Kvalsund, 2000, p. 411). He quotes a Norwegian student who underlines the unexpected loss of stature at transfer: 'Think of it, here we are, used to being the oldest – and after the summer holidays, hey presto, we're the youngest' (*ibid.*, p. 412). Such feelings are echoed in Morrison's recent interviews with new Year 7s in an East Anglian school (2000, p. 47) where the images they use to communicate their feelings are about size:

> I was used to being the biggest in the school but now I had shrunk. [And] there were about 200 people waiting round the bus stop – this was a big change compared to my 59 pupil school. (Y7, f)

> All the pupils seemed really large. I thought I was going to suffocate. (Y7, f)

> I felt like an ant in the middle of a football pitch. (Y7, m)

Underlying the surface concerns are more deep-rooted anxieties about status and identity in a different social setting and among teachers and peers that the newcomers are keen to impress. The new pupils' status as novices is exposed by their uncertainty about the rules in their new school, as one explains: 'You can take your coat or bag into the dining room at lunch time unless you're sandwiches and then you can take your bag in but not your coat – so you have to leave your coat [somewhere]' (Rudduck *et al.*, 1996, p. 21). There's also a different order of risk in the big school that they have to come to terms with: 'In our old school there was no troubles, with people not really stealing anything. Just like some people took like chocolate biscuits out of lunch boxes' – but in the new school ' people nick everything' (*ibid.*, p. 20). And if there are things that they miss from their primary school days – such as particular pastimes during break – they have to disguise their yearnings in the interest of protecting their new status, as Kvalsund points out: playing is something that belongs to the past; it is something you did before, but not now and certainly not in the playground during break:

> If the desire to play becomes too great to bear and you cannot help yourself, then it has to be done in secret and in a way that merges with the social landscape. Play must be camouflaged, so that the 'hawks' in the flock do not discover it. (2000, p. 417)

Transfer produces a cocktail of strong emotions, not just anxiety, and some impressions were still sharply etched on the minds of the pupils we interviewed a year or more later. What struck us in listening to the recorded interviews – and has subsequently influenced the direction of a national project on transfer – was that pupils talked animatedly about the size of the new school, its grounds, its resources, its equipment – but not so much about the learning. We asked what the advantages of being in the secondary school were – most of the replies were to do with things non-academic:

> There's trampolining, badminton, climbing and things like that.

> We're using nets [for basketball] instead of [in our old school] someone standing on a chair pretending to be a basket.

> At primary school we started at a quarter to nine and now we start at nine so we can stay in bed a bit longer. (Rudduck *et al.*, 1996, p. 23)

The transfer project's research team concluded that the excellent work that schools had done on easing the turbulence of transfer is now well established and indeed, the anxieties tend to be short term, fading as students get to know their way around. If there are still some weaknesses in the induction experiences, then the pupils can identify them *and* suggest improvements. (For example, Year 7 pupils interviewed by Mary Berry as part of the Transfer and Transition Project proposed a team task, using a map, to help new pupils find their way round school; and for learning the names of your new classmates they thought that pupils should take it in turns to call the register for the first few weeks.)

Meeting pupils' expectations about learning
Given that broadly effective induction arrangements for Year 7s have been achieved in many schools what is needed now, according to data from the Galton *et al.* study (2003), is more sustained attention to learning. This work, based on testing and interviews, shows why progress can dip, post-transfer, in some subjects. Student comments highlight the gap between the pre-transfer 'taster' sessions, especially in science, which can serve as a kind of recruitment bait ('in secondary we are going to do dangerous things, like experiments') and the more routine lessons, with work sheets and copying off the board, that they actually get after the first couple of weeks in their new school and that prove to be the mainstay of lessons. The Galton *et al.* report recommends that schools give more emphasis not only to sustaining a careful balance of challenge and support in learning post-transfer but also to strategies for helping pupils learn how to learn and how to manage their own learning: students want to feel that learning in the secondary school is not a repeat performance of what they did in

Year 6 but something that is taking them forward in more advanced and adult ways.

Although teachers may share this aspiration, the reality of transfer can make it difficult to realize. Teachers can find themselves dealing with a range of prior experiences and capabilities among the new intake and their priority may well be bringing pupils who are struggling up to speed on the basic skills – even though this may lead to more competent pupils feeling bored and disappointed that the promise of more exciting work has not materialized. Again, some primary schools make a strong commitment to developing confidence among young learners in talking about learning so that pupils, on transfer, already have the foundations of a meta-language for thinking about their own progress. However, given the range of primary schools that most secondaries now recruit from it is difficult for teachers to identify and build on the innovative practices of a few of their feeder schools. In the present climate, attention is more likely to be given to passing over the achievement data than to finding out how pupils have been trained to think about and talk abut their own learning.

So, one of the key issues in the current debate about progress post-transfer – the balancing of the social and academic – has been put more firmly on the agenda as a result of pupils' accounts of their experiences. Another transfer issue where pupil perspectives challenge received wisdom and practice is the balance between continuity and discontinuity. Whereas policy makers seem bent on smoothing out the bumps of transfer and see continuity as an unquestioned virtue, students seem to like discontinuity – or rather discontinuity-with-support – because it marks their move to a new stage of their school career and life course. At the moment teachers rely on bridging units which link the work of primary and secondary classrooms but some pupils complain in interview at having to complete Year 6 work in Year 7 when they expected that they had left the world of the primary school behind.

Understanding and adapting to the variety of teachers

A third issue highlighted indirectly by pupils (i.e. there is a stronger element of researcher interpretation) is the lack of explanation of some aspects of secondary schooling that are so familiar to teachers that their strangeness for pupils tends to be overlooked. The most striking example is the variety of teachers pupils encounter in the secondary school on a daily basis. There's a sense of 'the drunkenness of things being various' (as MacNeice put it), especially in relation to this great blooming of teachers – 'There's one who prods you, one who swears a bit, one who goes red in the face, one who's soft and nice.' The variety can also bring benefits, as one Year 7 explained with the wisdom of hindsight: 'It's more interesting, isn't it – used to be just sat in one classroom listening to one teacher blabbering on all day ... used to be boring' (Rudduck *et al.*, 1996, p. 23). In the recent past, pupils in English primary schools have been mainly taught by one teacher – the class teacher – in their *own* classroom. As subject specialization increases in primary schools, so the situation is changing. Nonetheless, a fairly major change for most pupils when they go to secondary school is that they move round the school and encounter a lot of different teachers, subjects and classrooms. Jenny Shaw points out (1995, p. 103) that as students move from elementary to secondary school the differences in organization 'are nearly always viewed as simply practical arrangements, the costs and benefits of larger institutions'. But their significance is greater, she claims, for 'teaching moves away from being organized around a whole person towards the more specialized and fragmented notion of the subject' and this is a major step in the process which socializes young people into the structuring of school knowledge. An experience of wholeness is fractured; they are being introduced to the principles of fragmentation and division which will intensify as students move on through secondary school.

Whereas in the early years of secondary school the student's world is built around the idea that 'teacher equals subject', later they may find, usually with little or no explanation, that they are being taught a subject by *two* teachers. They will have experienced something of this before when they change teachers at the end of a year or when a student or supply teacher replaces their usual teacher but these are *sequential* rather than *simultaneous* experiences. And although this is a rare experience for students aged 11 to 13, when it does occur, they are disoriented. As Jenny Shaw said, where explanations *are* offered, they tend to be about expediency – the problems of staffing or timetabling – and students tend to respond in terms of expediency, complaining that having two teachers for a subject means twice as much homework. But what students are actually encountering is another shift in their view of knowledge. As Shaw says, 'Being taught different subjects by different people clearly changes the meaning of learning.' The students' experience of a comfortable unity is gone: not only does the *subject* now become fractured – for the teachers probably have different specialisms – but they may also teach differently and think differently, and the student may not yet have been helped to deal with differences of style or opinion *within* the subject. These transitions – from one teacher to many and from one teacher per subject to several – are bewildering to some students, but over time they are likely to be socialized into accepting the arbitrariness and strangeness of some of the things that happen in school.

If, as we suggested earlier, the move to secondary school is an opportunity to help pupils think about learning and about themselves as learners, then it is important that they are able to understand purposes and processes and also feel confident enough to ask questions about the things that they don't understand rather than sit on their uncertainties like eggs that are never going to hatch.

Understanding and adjusting to homework
One area of relatively unfamiliar experience for transfer pupils is homework. Not all students in primary school, even now, are used to doing homework on a regular basis and not all are clear about why they do it and how it relates to work done in school. Moreover, the growth of after-school study support facilities means that although the term 'homework' is still used, it can mean different things in different schools. After the move to the big school, according to our interviews, many pupils respond positively to homework, seeing it as a symbol of advancement in their school careers, but the excitement may not last and if it is not well managed pupils lose faith and start to develop specific work-avoidance strategies. In one school – this was not a typical response nationally but it is indicative of the need to explore pupils' constructions of meaning in different contexts – some pupils saw homework as a mark of teacher incompetence: if the teacher did not manage to complete what he or she planned to do in class then the pupils 'got lumbered' with finishing it off at

home. Other pupils saw it as evidence of teachers' vindictiveness – setting 'noddy' tasks that pupils were obliged to do and then not bothering to mark the work.

One of the problems from the teacher's perspective is that homework tasks tend now to be formally scheduled and written in planners for parents to see and monitor. Where parents take the task of surveillance seriously it reflects badly on the school if homework is not set. Martin Hughes and colleagues, in their recent study for the Economic and Social Research Council (ESRC), highlighted the symbolic function of homework in parents' judgments of 'a good school': an emphasis on homework was seen as something which was associated with a 'good' school, in much the same way that school uniform often is:

> It's one of these old catchwords isn't it? It has a sort of resonance, a sort of ring to it ... 'We know what it's about, it's about standards and decency and the empire and all that kind of stuff.' And I think it's one of these words that people use as a kind of code for the kind of school they expect. The word homework means an ordered community where expectations are high, where our children are supported. That's its importance as a code word and that's why I think parents want it. (A headteacher, in Hughes, 2002)

Where such attitudes prevail, the pressure is on teachers to set something rather than nothing – hence the complaint that some tasks are 'noddy'.

Pupils are also quick to suss out which teachers don't take homework seriously and they react accordingly; one Year 9 said proudly that he had stopped doing homework for some teachers early in Year 8 and only worked hard for those teachers whose classes he liked or who were reliable about marking. What pupils don't realize is that if they do not develop a reasonable competence in managing learning outside the supervised lesson then they may well have great difficulties later in coping with the multiple demands of course work and revision. In a sense some pupils are unconsciously conspiring in the construction of their own disadvantage.

Hughes's report suggests, importantly, that three things should be given more attention: explanation of the different purposes of homework tasks; strategies for setting about 'revision' homework which many pupils had trouble with; and the more regular provision of useful feedback rather than just ticks or grades.

Understanding and adjusting to the new secondary school

One of the issues threading through this section on transfer is the importance of helping pupils understand what learning in the secondary school is, how it differs from learning in the primary school, and how the secondary school is organized. Bucannan-Barrow and Barrett (1996, p. 34) describe new pupils as 'relatively powerless strangers':

> The school is an extensive system, with many of its workings, structure and power patterns invisible and unexplained to the young pupil. It is, in microcosm, a multi-faceted and multi-layered society and presents a considerable interpretative problem for children. And yet, for successful functioning, the young pupil needs to have an understanding of the interconnectedness of such aspects as rules, roles, power and community.

The authors suggest that patterns of social interaction that pupils develop in school, often without a working knowledge of how rules, roles, power and authority connect up, 'may well have an enduring influence on their participation in other social contexts, even into adulthood'.

In conclusion we would say that it is no easy task for young people to establish good work habits for alongside the development of the self-as-learner there is the need to develop the social self and the sexual self and the three can often represent competing priorities. White reminds us (1971, p. 340) that institutional life is and has to be highly organized and that it is all too easy, post-transfer, for the 'daily chores, the demands, the inspections' – as well as the regular devices for work avoidance – to 'become the reality' and not the larger purposes of schooling. And so it is only when the significance of those larger purposes confront students – as they do in Year 10 when exams loom large – that they see the importance of building up reliable work habits. As adults and as teachers it is so much easier for us than it is for students to see where learning is going and how important it is to establish a commitment to the seriousness of learning early on in their secondary school careers – without in any way curbing the vitality and spirit of their social explorations.

In the next section we summarize what we learnt from pupils about Years 3 and 8 where Ofsted inspections have reported on dips in progress.

The Year 8 and Year 3 'dips'

From the early 1990s the Chief Inspector's Annual Reports included tables which showed a sustained 'dip' in progress at Year 3 and at Year 8. In both cases the tendency was to blame poor teaching.

Our interviews with Year 8 pupils, which pre-dated the publicity surrounding the Ofsted analysis, suggested that the situation was more complicated than that. We checked out our interview data with Year 8 and Year 9 pupils in different schools in different parts of the country and found a high degree of consistency in pupils' perceptions of Year 8. This account brings together data from Year 8 pupils in three northern secondary schools (see Rudduck *et al.*, 1996); data from eight Cambridge and Lincolnshire schools (see Rudduck *et al.*, 1998); and data from one Essex school (see Galton *et al.*, 2003). To distinguish the three data sets, the report dates are given in brackets.

Ofsted reports also indicated a dip in pupils' performance in Year 3, at the start of Key Stage 2. The basis of the judgement – as with the judgments of performance in Year 8 – was the lower percentage of *individual lessons* observed, compared with similar figures for other years, in which pupils appeared to be making acceptable progress. The extent to which judgments about progress in the individual lessons can be used as proxy for overall pupil progress has been questioned (for a critique, see Richards, 2001). Nonetheless, the Ofsted data have served an important purpose in highlighting an issue that warranted a more detailed investigation. In 1998 a team based in Cambridge (led by Doddington and Flutter) launched an interview-based investigation, *Sustaining Pupils' Progress at Year 3*, which was supported with a small grant from Ofsted. The aim was to open up the factors behind the Year 3 dip through the perspectives of those most closely involved – pupils and teachers. Working with a group of schools in two local education authorities in the south and east of England the project built up an extensive database of interview evidence.

Here we show how, by taking account of pupils' perceptions and experiences, we can build up a more realistic picture of what is happening at these two important moments in young people's school careers.

The Year 8 dip: what we learnt from pupils

Data from pupil interviews for an ESRC study (see Rudduck *et al.*, 1996) suggest that there are 'twin peaks' in pupils' engagement – at Years 7 and 11. In Year 7 pupils' attention is captured by the social novelties of the new school: most pupils are caught up in the excitement of exploring new spaces ('it's very easy to get lost'), new opportunities ('more things to do in the breaks'), and a wider range of facilities (drinks machines) and resources (astro-turf, computers). Learning (other than social learning) can be overshadowed by the excitements and social risks of 'the big school'. Engagement peaks again in Years 10 and 11 but this time it is driven by the need to get good grades and for many pupils it is sustained through anxiety and stress.

What is missing for many pupils between the two high points of engagement is a clear understanding of what learning leads to and how later learning builds on earlier learning, not only in terms of content but also in terms of ways of working. This may not be surprising given that each year of secondary schooling is fenced off and made relatively self-contained. The problem is compounded, as the interview data showed, by the lack of a clear and compelling identity for the second year of secondary school – Year 8. We asked Year 9 pupils to sum up each year of secondary school as they had experienced it or as they had anticipated it. Year 8 proved to be a nondescript year: in the first quotation, Year 8 is not mentioned; in the second, it is mentioned but has no distinctive purpose:

> In Year 7 it's all new, in Year 9 you are doing your options, in Year 10 you are starting your GCSEs and in Year 11 you are there. (1996)

> Year 8 is the year between Year 7 and SATs. (1998)

> Year 8 is the easy year. This is because you're already settled in ... It's the only real year when you get a rest. (2003)

There are no obvious challenges in Year 8 that Year 7 pupils can look forward to – except those that individual schools construct. This is the time when routine sets in, when engagement can flag:

> You think, 'Oh God! I've got this today!' and so on. It gets really boring and you don't feel excited any more coming to school. (1996)

> Year 7 you have just moved from a different school and in Year 8 you have already been there and you have nothing important to think about. (1998)

> Year 7 is getting used to the school and teachers where Year 8 is very laid back in that sense. (1998)

> Our problem with Year 8 is that there is nothing new to do. (2003)

Year 8 is a year which teachers think will look after itself but in fact it is, for pupils, a relatively featureless year – one that needs rescuing and given a positive learning-oriented identity.

In our earlier interviews we collated what pupils were saying in different settings and built up a picture of Year 8 from the pupil perspective. Later we were able to discuss 'the problem of Year 8' directly with pupils (2003) and we found that not only did they understand but they could also come up with good ideas about ways of marking the move to another year. Mary Berry explained to a class of Year 8 pupils in a fairly high-achieving secondary boys' school about the Year 8 dip, and whether they recognized it and what might be done about it. Responses were discussed in pairs, then drafted as a joint commentary on the computer. The first statement, from a very articulate pupil, offers a brief analysis of the problem as well as a range of solutions; on the whole the suggestions are more to do with social markers of seniority than with ways of making learning more engaging:

> Year 8 pupils also need an identity, as without it, the year can seem just a boring repeat of the year before, and the students may not perform as well. To do this, schools need to give Year 8s more responsibility. They could do this by making them show prospective Year 7s around the school, and acting as 'buddies' for new pupils. Perhaps e-mailing a new student before they arrive could enhance this. Another way of giving the Year 8s more identity may be to slightly alter the uniform, thus they would appear different to the other years as well. These

changes could be simply a different coloured tie, a special badge on their blazers, or something more major, such as wearing polo shirts instead of normal shirts. Perhaps giving Year 8s a wider range of subjects may also increase their identity. Giving them subjects that they did not study in Year 7 would make them feel more privileged, and might make them work slightly better. (2003, Y8, b)

Other pupils also focused on status solutions, using uniform as a way of marking out membership of an older year group:

Perhaps a change of tie for the Year 8s would make us more recognized. At the moment, Year 8 is just the year between 7 and 9, but nothing more. (2003, Y8, b)

As completely changing the uniforms each year would [money-wise] disagree with parents and no uniform would be unruly [*sic*], I have come up with a plan. If on each blazer there was a strip of Velcro, each year pupils could buy a different coloured braid/strip to signify their year – gradually getting lighter or darker towards the end of school. This would suit everyone. (2003, Y8, b)

There was a particularly plaintive statement from a Year 8 boy who clearly suffered because of his small stature:

Have a slight difference in the uniform, not so much that it's expensive but just tie colour or something. This would help differentiate us (especially the smaller amongst us) from the Year 7 students. (2002, Y8, b)

These were all ideas, from pupils, about making Year 8 different and more important. From a relatively early age pupils develop their own views of what matters in school – interpreting the messages that they hear from teachers, from parents, from the media. The consequence is that they may choose to minimize their effort in years that they see as less important and thereby unwittingly limit later progress and achievement. The national concern to raise standards can lead people to think that education in secondary schools is about little more than tests and examinations, and pupil perceptions of 'the stuff that counts' is coloured by such assumptions. By reinforcing the impression that the Year 11 examinations are what *really* matters schools may be giving unintended messages to pupils that the earlier years *don't* matter so much – that they are 'on the back burner' years:

Once you get to Year 9 I think that is where it starts getting more important. (1998)

It's like end of fourth year and beginning of fifth year you start doing stuff that counts; it's got nowt to do with first, second or third. (1996)

I always feel like – Oh I shouldn't be working this hard because it is only Year 8. (1998)

Some headteachers have said that they usually put their most experienced teachers with the top sets and/or with the examination groups; they also think about which teachers are good with Year 7 pupils. But is seems that relatively little attention is given to the kind of teacher that Year 8s need or to styles of teaching and learning that will challenge them and sustain their engagement ('We get all the naff teachers in Year 8'). Where mentoring schemes were originally introduced to support pupils at risk of disengaging they were more likely to focus on Year 10 and 11 pupils in order to boost their examination grades through short-term support strategies. In our view it is educationally more acceptable to look out for evidence of disengagement early in pupils' school careers and provide support that will sustain a longer-term commitment. By the end of Year 7 pupils are ready for new challenges; if they are not stretched and excited by the academic content of lessons then their attention can turn away from learning. Some pupils said that in Year 8:

[School work] feels the same [level of] difficulty it was a year ago. (1996)

You've done some of it in Year 7. Year 8 work is not too difficult; it is more or less the same. (1998)

Year 8 seems to be a pivotal year when pupils need to be helped to think and act strategically in relation to their learning and to understand how a commitment to learning now can enhance life chances. At the same time schools need to ensure that they are sustaining the view, in all they say and do, that *Year 8 matters*.

Another thread in the story of Year 8, as it emerged from the interviews, is that pupils, no longer the youngest in the school, feel less raw and vulnerable – although one advantage is that 'the older pupils lay off you and start on the new Year 7s' (1998). Pupils are conscious of 'growing up'. They would like teachers to recognize that they are a year older; they value occasions when they are given responsibility, whether for hearing a younger pupil read or helping to organize a fund-raising activity. They like special events and trips (these often involve an element of challenge and self-direction). A common feeling across the schools was that 'Teachers should listen to us more, hear what we've got to say' (1998). If their aspiration 'to be treated like an adult' is not recognized and respected, they may seek 'respect' within the peer-group, and the desire for esteem may be expressed in bullying or through focusing on behaviours and activities that readily win acclaim from their mates but that can, in some circumstances, endorse an 'it's not cool to learn' culture.

We also learned from talking to pupils that for many a tension starts to build up in Years 7 and 8 between the pull of the peer group and the demands of school work. The strength of 'anti-boffin' peer pressure can make it difficult for individual pupils to be seen to commit themselves to 'academic' learning. While recognizing that pupils gain a sense of identity by taking on the values of a group of peers, the school needs to take steps to establish a culture where *all* pupils feel that it is acceptable to learn and where individual pupils have support in establishing a positive sense of self-as-learner.

The significance of what we learned from pupils is underlined by Anderman and Maehr's review of research on motivation and schooling (1994). Overall, they say, 'the literature supports the view of decreased investment [by pupils] in academic activities and increased investment in non-academic activities during the middle grades' (p. 288):

> Issues of motivation have a degree of uniqueness and a special sense of urgency about them [at this time]. The motivation of adolescents is a critical issue – it is, in fact, a problem that must be solved. (Anderman and Maehr, 1994, pp. 287–8)

Motivation affects achievement and this is the period when patterns of achievement can, for a minority of pupils, open up or close down particular pathways to careers:

School investment during the middle [years] may have serious and enduring effects on shaping career patterns and life choices. That this lack of investment all too often eventuates in dropping out of school before [the examinations] is disturbing, if not frightening. (*ibid.*, p. 289)

It is easy to accept these problems as the product of adolescence which we can do nothing about except hope that pupils will pass safely through the turbulence. Our argument, however, is that there *are* things that can be done to sustain pupils' commitment to learning. Anderman and Maehr share this view, suggesting that tasks which challenge and engage pupils, and help them to think things out for themselves, are more satisfying than tasks which are 'performance'-oriented – that is, tasks which seek short-term goals and rely on surface-level strategies, such as copying things down. They claim that explanations for the 'disturbing downturn in motivation at this time' (p. 288) lie largely in the mismatch between the environment of learning in the school (broadly conceived) and pupils' 'heightened awareness of emerging adulthood'. Early adolescence, they say, is a period when autonomy, self-determination and social-interaction are very important for young people (p. 294). However, the typical school environment of the middle years has relatively few opportunities for pupils to make important decisions (hence, in our research, the significance for pupils of options choices, however restricted, towards the end of Year 9). Anderman and Maehr are reporting on education in the United States but Hirsch confirms (1998, p. 70) that in many European countries schooling at this stage is 'similarly seen as a weak link in the educational system'. The distinctive contribution of Anderman and Maehr's review is the bringing together of issues of school organization, motivation and performance – a relationship that our own research has also highlighted.

In summary, our interview data allowed us to construct a fuller picture of what can go wrong in Year 8:

- the impact on pupils' motivation of Year 8 having no clear identity in their eyes;
- the examination work (i.e. Years 10 and 11) being presented, and seen, as being 'the stuff that counts' in school;

- the need to give an identity to each year so that pupils' commitment to what lies ahead can be sustained across the chasm of the long summer break;
- the widespread failure to acknowledge pupils' social maturity and their mood for more responsibility as they move through the different years of school;
- the low priority given in staffing to the kind of teacher that Year 8 needs.

What might schools do to sustain pupils' commitment to learning and make Year 8 special? Here are some strategies that schools have used to enable them to give Year 8 a lift:

- Giving a clear learning-oriented identity, and more status, to Year 8, and ensuring that there are things that Year 7 pupils look forward to. (For example, inviting pupils to plan an autumn event for parents that shows how their work has developed this year and what is distinctive about being in Year 8.)
- Making sure that the teaching in Year 8 provides opportunities for active participation. (For example, identifying tasks where learning can appropriately be pursued through discussion in groups and through problem-solving.)
- Creating time for dialogue about learning so that pupils begin to understand the longer-term implications of what they are doing and also begin to develop a language for thinking about learning and about themselves as learners.
- Introducing a mentoring scheme (with older or younger pupils) that makes Year 8 pupils feel special and helps them to talk openly about problems with learning.
- Identifying opportunities for Year 8 pupils to exercise responsibility in ways that mark their moving up into the second year of secondary schooling and no longer being the youngest in the school.
- Strengthening the procedures and practices relating to homework (or study support) so that pupils learn, early in their secondary school career, the importance of being able to work independently and to pace themselves outside the time-frame set by the length of school lessons.

- Responding to the problem of 'catching up' for pupils who have missed work, whether through illness or choice. If pupils gain the impression in Year 8 that it doesn't matter to miss sequences of learning they may find that later on they do not have a strong enough scaffolding for more advanced work.
- Monitoring the messages that the school is giving about the status of Year 8 and Year 8 work.

If Year 7 is characterized by the process of initiation into a new social context and new ways of learning, Year 8 needs to be marked by opportunities for greater responsibility and creativity, occasions for thinking and talking about learning, and for establishing skills of organization and self-direction in readiness for the decision-making of Year 9 and the pressures of Years 10 and 11. Pupils who do not build good foundations at this stage, in terms of ways of working and subject knowledge, can find later that they have left things too late and that it is easier to give up than to try to catch up

*The Year 3 dip: what have we learnt from pupils?**
Although Year 8 and Year 3 had both been identified as points where pupils' learning appeared to slow down, we were aware that these two periods represent distinctly different stages in pupils' school careers. Year 8, as we have argued, represents a somewhat 'fallow' period between the excitement of transfer (Year 7) and the 'important' test and examination years (Years 9 to 11) whereas Year 3 marks the step-over point between the first two Key Stages of the National Curriculum when pupils and teachers have to adjust to a new set of teaching and learning demands. In some cases, of course, Year 3 can also be a point of transfer where pupils move from infant to junior school with all the attendant excitements and uncertainties of becoming part of a new physical and social environment.

What did we learn from pupils about their perceptions and experiences of the move to Year 3? First, unlike the Year 8 situation, pupils were keenly aware that the move to Year 3 was important.

---

* Note: the data for this section were collected by Doddington and colleagues and reported in Doddington *et al.*, 2001, and Bearne, 2002.

They talked about their 'advancement' in social as well as academic terms; the transition to 'being more senior' was clearly recognized and appreciated.

Even as going to school is an important step away from childhood, so the move to Year 3 is another big step forward – and pupils often have high expectations. Some lines from a poem on a school notice-board (author unknown) capture a five-year old's disappointment when expectations were not realized:

> My first day at school today. / Funny sort of day.

> Didn't seem to learn much. / Seemed all we did was play.

The young student expected school to be different from home – to be about working hard to learn. Similarly, in Year 3 there were many positive responses to the social and academic markers of being in the next stage of education:

> We have to think for ourselves sometimes. (Y3, b)

> In Year 3 you can do more things, you're not treated like little kids, you're treated more grownup-ly and you don't have to be shown about because we can look after ourselves. (Y3, b)

> I've noticed something – in Year 2 we didn't count up to 100 because she thought it was too hard and in Year 3 I just sort of learned it straight away. (Y3, g)

> [Now we're juniors] we have to call our speech marks just actual speech marks and in the infants we could call them 66s and 99s but we have to use the proper word now . . . (Y3, b)

Teachers were clear that the work *was* more demanding in Year 3 and pupils' comments bore this out, although some revealed an anxious sense of strain:

> Well, last year I found it a bit easy but now we're up here it's a bit harder and I don't know what to do. (Y3, b)

> You have to like get [the work] done in 25 minutes or 45 minutes and it's really hard, hard work. (Y3, b)

> Well, you have loads more writing than in Year 2. (Y3, g)

The thing I don't like about one of my lessons is the maths because we always have to do like complicated things and it's a bit awkward. (Y3, g)

Sometimes I don't like English because bits of it are too hard – everyday it gets a tiny bit harder. There's too much writing. (Y3, b)

The strain may reflect the pressure on Key Stage 2 teachers who see their task as very different from that of Year 2 teachers, in terms of both academic and personal development:

In Year 2 they're molly-coddled and they can get a lot of attention whereas now, in Year 3, they have to cope on their own more. (Y3 teacher)

Teachers are aware of the difficulties that some of their pupils are experiencing in adjusting: 'They get worried and say that they "have a lot of work"; ... we expect more sustained pieces of writing and some of them find that a bit daunting.' But the learning curve may be too steep for some young students.

Another factor in the fall-off in progress may be, as we learnt from the interviews, that parents who hear that pupils must be more independent in Year 3 and that the work will be harder may offer less support – either because they feel the content is beyond them or because they feel that pupils should be learning to work without their help. There is also the issue of the quality of teaching: some headteachers in the project acknowledged, as in the case of Year 8, that Year 3 was where they 'hid' their weaker teachers. But the dip in progress cannot just be attributed to poor teaching; as we have seen, the situation is more complex than that and needs to be looked at and understood taking into account the perspective of the pupils themselves.

Schools which have a clear awareness of what the transition can mean for pupils can plan support strategies to help them cope with the new demands while at the same time they can enjoy the satisfaction of being a year older and doing more advanced work. For example, we found that where schools gave careful consideration to introducing and explaining new aspects of learning required by the Key Stage 2 curriculum, pupils across the ability range were more confident and robust. In contrast, where liaison between

Year 2 and 3 teachers was haphazard and where there was no systematic preparation for what lay ahead, less confident learners could easily lose ground in the face of new expectations about the quantity and quality of their work. Some pupils, at this early stage in their school careers, were beginning to see learning as a burdensome struggle and there were expressions of self-doubt and anxiety.

As Woods points out, negative views of learning, acquired early on in pupils' school careers, can have serious, long-term repercussions:

> Life-chances are determined or constructed for many people in the early years. The channels of their educational potential which is realised at secondary school are already formulated before they arrive there … the 7–8 age group is a crucial one in the development of those attitudes, abilities and relationships that go into the making of educational success at that level. In this sense the transition is not only of infant to junior. Like joined-up writing and the second set of teeth, there are other ultimates here, and they lay down the means for the next transfer to secondary, and indeed for later life. (1987, p. 120; in Doddington *et al.*, 2001)

Listening to what pupils had to say about their experiences as learners enabled us to construct a chart of the pros and cons of Year 3 and highlight some of the problematic organisational issues that teachers and schools may need to work on to support pupils at this crucial point of transition (see Table below).

Table: Some key themes and their potential impact on pupils' progress

PROGRESS DIPS	an example of negative outcome	THEME	an example of positive outcome	PROGRESS SUSTAINED
⇩	Pupils find difficulty in coping with the expectation of working more independently.	**INDEPENDENCE AND RESPONSIBILITY**	Pupils enjoy new approaches offering greater independence and responsibility.	⇧

PROGRESS DIPS	an example of negative outcome	THEME	an example of positive outcome	PROGRESS SUSTAINED
⇩	Increased curricular demands lead to pressure and can result in some pupils falling behind.	THE CURRICULUM	The new phase offers challenge and enhances motivation for learning.	⇧
⇩	Pupils are unfamiliar with new ways of working and have difficulty in coping with them.	WAYS OF WORKING	New ways of working offer variety and help pupils to develop useful skills for collaborative learning.	⇧
⇩	Pupils' anxiety about assessment depress self-esteem and lead to a loss of confidence.	MONITORING & ASSESSMENT	Effective monitoring highlights problems so that they can be quickly addressed.	⇧
⇩	A fall-off in parental involvement in Y3 means some pupils receive less support.	THE HOME DIMENSION	Parents given information on Y3 and KS2 so they can offer appropriate support.	⇧
⇩	School leadership does not recognize the distinctiveness of Y3 and places weaker teachers in this year.	SCHOOL ORGANIZATION & STAFFING	In allocating staff to Y3, school leadership gives attention to the particular Y3 needs.	⇧

PROGRESS DIPS	an example of negative outcome	THEME	an example of positive outcome	PROGRESS SUSTAINED
⇩	Limited Y2/Y3 liaison leads to problems being overlooked, such as pupil under-performance.	**YEAR 2/YEAR 3 LIAISON**	Detailed information passed on by Y2 teachers helps Y3 teachers to sustain pupils' progress.	⇧

Reproduced from Doddington *et al.*, 2001, p.14

Comment: The importance of marking social progression

From the adult perspective the path of learning is relatively straight-forward: pupils move through the different years of schooling, building up a resource of knowledge, understanding and skills which provides a foundation for tackling the next, more advanced stage of work. An expectation of progress is built into the sequence of transitions within and across schools and it is what gives structure to the national curriculum and its related programme of assessment.

A common structuring device in schools in the UK is the annual advance of the whole age cohort (from Year 7 to Year 8, from Year 8 to Year 9, and so on). But while we give a lot of attention to academic progress and the way the curriculum changes as pupils move up through the different years of schooling, we give less thought to the ways in which their increasing sense of adultness needs to be acknowledged and marked.

As we have seen, Year 6 students have strong expectations that reflect the symbolic importance of the transfer from primary to secondary school. But the move up from Year 7 to Year 8, within the same school, is not widely marked by schools in terms of an increase in more 'adult' responsibilities and relationships.

Alongside the concern to gain individual respect within the status systems operated by the school and the students is the concern of the year group as a whole to be treated in ways that match their increased maturity as they move through the institutional time frame. Being a year older matters, whether you are 7 or 13, and it seems important to find ways of acknowledging young people's expectations in relation to learning as well as in relation to their sense of self. Our data suggests that for each new academic year a more explicit marking of age and responsibility could help stem the drift towards disengagement.

There has, of course, been a strong convention of marking the seniority of the oldest pupils in the school by giving them regulatory responsibilities as prefects, for instance, or by giving them spatial privileges, such as their own common room. But pupils want some recognition earlier in their school careers – as this Year 8 boy explains (he is from a boys' school – hence his male-centred view of the possibilities):

> Responsibility is something that a lot of children would like, but usually it is kept until the sixth form. Titles like head boy of year would fulfil this request quite well but there should be more, as only one would leave a lot of people jealous. (2002)

How schools respect young people's age in the organizational frameworks of schooling is an important dimension of pupils' feelings of membership. As James and Prout said, '. . . it is during childhood that age has a particular significance' (1997, p. 234). And Kvalsund, from Norway, comments: 'Becoming one year older, moving up one form, is socially important among pupils in the Norwegian schools. The pupils encounter different modes of access to valued resources and new social rights and new obligations' (2000, p. 402). Indeed, age is part of the basic logic of school organization – it is another dividing practice (Meadmore, 1993) and operates in relation to social spaces as well as affecting the interactions between members of the school community. It is interesting that one side-effect of peer mentoring schemes and student as researcher initiatives is the breaking down of segregation by age.

Given that schooling is organized in a way that makes 'childhood into a very specific kind of age-graded condition' (Hendrick, 1997, p. 35) it is somewhat surprising that we think about progression more in terms of the curriculum than young people's status in and contribution to the community of the school. Being able to manage the tension between the social and academic strands of one's life is an important accomplishment for young people. And, again, it is through listening to pupils that we have come to realize the importance of this dimension of their experience and the way it can colour their attitude to school and their motivation to learn.

*

In the next section we look at what pupils who find learning a struggle say about the things that shape their confidence as learners. Their stories suggest some ways in which policy makers and practitioners can intervene to ensure that they can build and sustain a more positive sense of self.

The Individual Dimension

Behind the bravado and nonchalance which some students wear like bulletproof vests to protect themselves from loss of dignity (see Chaplain, 1996, pp. 102–5) most students we interviewed wanted to do well and make something of their lives. But somewhere in the twilight zone between myth and reality they had constructed a view of the school, its status passages, and their position in it – and for some the view was discouraging. Their images of self as learner were largely shaped by the messages that the school transmitted, often unwittingly. And at the same time, teachers had constructed pictures of pupils and their reputations and it was often the fixed nature of these images that made it difficult for pupils to think that change was possible.

In this section, drawing on pupils' accounts of their experiences as learners, we discuss some of the things that structure and sustain poor self-image in school. We also look at the problem of changing your image. Framing the discussion is the recognition that the institutionalized nature of learning makes it difficult, however generously teachers give time to pupils, for all pupils to feel that they are understood and supported as individuals. As they get older they seem to feel the need to emerge from the routines of schooling and from the anonymity (to use Stevie Smith's words) of being 'only one of many / And of small account if any'. They want to feel that they matter. These feelings were as strong in our data as they were in the surveys carried out in Scotland 25 years before, in the late 1970s:

> [Mr X] showed the greatest interest in all the pupils and made you feel like a real person. (Male school leaver, CES data, 1978)

> Teachers should take a deep interest in each separate person. (Female school leaver, CES data, 1978)

> Once the exams have been completed ... you feel as if you are a hindrance to the up and coming pupils. It is a crucial stage of your life leaving school [but some teachers feel] that their work [on you] is finished. (Male school leaver, CES data, 1978)

Knowing that you are a valued member of the school community is an important foundation for students' commitment to learning, but not all feel this. For instance, some Year 11 pupils told us they felt the school was not interested in them and their futures but only in their getting good grades to boost the school's reputation.

Positive and negative images of self-as-learner emerge in particular in the context of the dividing practices that proliferate in schools. In this section we look, from pupils' perspectives, at the arenas where such practices operate most sharply and at their influence on pupils' sense of self and engagement with learning. Some of our data suggests that we need, in particular, to consider whether we are conspiring in the self-protective withdrawal of some young people from situations where they think they will fail because they have come to see themselves as 'no good'.

The intensification of 'dividing practices' in schools

The structures of schooling are in many ways quite unlike the structures in which young people have to operate beyond school. The world of school is marked by practices that are so familiar that they cease to be strange – until we hear how pupils experience them. First, in a purely practical, organizational sense, schools could not operate at all without some system of segregation: so, pupils in our education system are sorted by age; curriculum content is parcelled out into tightly bounded subjects and teachers labelled accordingly, and the day is divided into chunks. These practices are relatively neutral in relation to the labelling of pupils. But other practices are not: they indicate to pupils that some are valued more than others. And those who are most highly valued may have access to better resources and opportunities.

Reba Page's study (1989) offers striking evidence of this. Families sending their children to Southmoor School in the USA were almost exclusively white middle- or upper-class and the pupil body was socially advantaged. There was almost total commitment to the ideal of an academic curriculum. Within the school there was, however, a small population of academically less successful pupils who nevertheless expressed their support for the school and what it stood for. These pupils followed a 'lower track' curriculum but one that was still designed to tackle academic content. The main difference between the lower track and the regular track curriculum was the pedagogy. In the regular classes, teachers promoted debate: 'Civil but serious intellectual exchanges were the currency' and students 'were expected to develop critical thinking skills … the teachers presented students with complex questions fairly dripping with controversy'. But in lower track classes, the possibility of disagreement was to a large extent avoided by a reliance on 'individual seat work, films, silent reading, and social activities'. The pupils 'were enjoined to think' but they were encouraged, unlike their regular track peers, 'to keep into the teacher's ideas' (p. 209). On those occasions where pupils managed to raise an issue that was on the margins of controversy, 'the disagreements … were rather quickly woven back into the on-going flow of talk'. In the lower tracks, debate was seen as a challenge to the authority of the teacher rather than, as in the regular tracks, an intellectual enquiry that pupils and teachers could pursue together. What the lower track pupils came to learn was that their contribution to the school was to stay out of the way of its 'main operation of academic pre-eminence' (p. 218).

The study powerfully highlights the dynamic of differentiation and the way it works: it disadvantages pupils, both individual and groups, to the extent that assumptions about their capability are made and sustained on their position within internal hierarchies – which may reflect social class (see Boaler *et al.*, 2000, p. 633).

The three sites of differentiation that we shall look at, from the pupil perspective, are grouping and setting, testing and 'selection' for transfer. A final section looks at the problems of changing the image that others in the school hold of you.

Grouping and setting*

> During the whole secondary school period it has been my main expectation to leave the class I am in. The fact that I am in the worst class of the school has made my study difficult. The greatest problem is that all study progresses according to the general level of the class. Thus all other classes have been able to study things that might prove useful for them in the long run, but that material we cannot cover. The wheat is separated from the chaff at secondary school (Finnish boy, grade 9, in Pietarinen, 2000, p. 395)

Either the boy quoted above is immensely restrained and courteous or the intensity of his feelings have been lost in the translation; nevertheless, his message is clear and it is similar to things we hear from young people in our own education system.

Pupils continue to comment on what they see as the divisiveness of the system, especially if they find themselves in 'bottom' groups for several subjects. In the past, schools have disguised the hierarchy of groups by claiming that they are about speed of work and not pupil ability, or that there is one advanced group and that all the rest are parallel. The use of colours or other supposedly 'neutral' terms is designed to support the deception. But pupils are not so easily taken in:

> Like all my mates are still in 'parallel group' as they call it, but everybody calls it duggy group. (Y9)

> We've got these groups, Jupiter, Mars, Venus, Earth and like, like the one I'm in they've got the lowest. They don't say they have but we think they have, don't we? ... because Jupiter have got all not very brainy ones. (Y9)

Top sets are seen as conferring certain advantages that other pupils are denied – whether to do with benefits beyond schooling ('If you're in the top group you've got a good chance of getting a better job',

---

* Note: in this section the pupil quotations, unless otherwise referenced, are from our earlier ESRC project, see Rudduck *et al.*, 1996.

Y8) or to do with the quality of teaching and learning ('It's easier to do your exam if you're in the top set than in bottom – you get a better education', Y8). There is some sense in this given the talk of constant messing about that characterizes the climate of some bottom sets. Interestingly – and reminiscent of the Reba Page story summarized above – some pupils think that you learn different and, by implication, better things in the top sets. Other comments reflect the order of significance in schools: where good grades matter for the school then pupils in the sets most likely to deliver the good grades are most important:

> The teachers concentrate more on you in top sets and not the people who are below you. (Y8)

> It's better to be [in the high sets] because you are thought better of by teachers. (Y9)

A simple logic then comes into play: if you know that the top set pupils count for most in school, get the best teachers, the best results and the best opportunities for the futures, then those not in the top sets have little basis for feeling good about themselves in relation to the school's academic purposes:

> [In the top set] you've got more confidence in yourself. Like if you're in the bottom set you ain't got no confidence. You think you're just going to fail. (Y8)

Such pupils, as we know, will seek self-esteem in school in other ways, perhaps by excelling in sporting activities or by enlisting the support of their peers in anti-work diversions.

However, despite the perceived benefits of a 'top group education' not all pupils aspire to be in the top sets, particularly if you have to read 'books that have a liking for complicated language' (Y10). Top sets are seen by some pupils as demanding *very* hard work which they think they won't manage or which they don't want to manage. The Year 9 students in Boaler *et al.*'s study of grouping practices in maths in six schools (2000) also reported 'top set' problems and the researchers made their own observations:

> In a range of top-set classes the teachers raced through examples on the board, speaking quickly, often interjecting their speech with

phrases such as 'Come on, we haven't got much time' and 'Just do this quickly'. (p. 635)

Some of the teachers also reprimanded students who said that they did not understand, adding comments such as 'You should be able to, you're in the top set'. (p. 635)

Some students in the top sets are protective of their image within the peer group and don't want to be seen by their mates as a 'working hard, top set' person ('I don't want to be in the top group because you get called boff', Y8). Moreover, some pupils have heard from their mates that there are hierarchies even within the top sets and they prefer to avoid the risk of embarrassment:

I think that certainly [in] the top sets they concentrate too much on the really intelligent people that they want to get A*s but they don't think about the other people [in that set] that might be struggling . . . and if you're asked a question which you don't understand everyone looks down at you – 'Oh, don't you know that kind of thing?' so I think it causes a lot of people to just sit there and just kind of worry about it on their own. (Y9)

Many of the comments quoted above, while ostensibly about the top sets, say something about the perceived disadvantage of life at the bottom. Some pupils think they are losing out: for example, the older sister of one pupil 'just missed' getting into the top set and the work she has in the next set 'is stupid; she brung her book home and it's stupid. It don't learn you nowt. It's completely simple' (Y8). Other pupils comment on the quality of the teachers assigned to the lower sets:

. . . people in like the lower group . . . don't learn nowt because of the teacher. He just writes stuff on the board and then gives you the answers straight away so they can't learn nothin. (Y9)

I mean teacher what we've got now he's not bothered, he don't encourage us to work and when everybody's messing about and shouting and bawling you can't work. (Y9)

Being in a low set can galvanize some pupils to try to get out ('I would like another test at the end of the year to see who can get in top group out of bottom group. And I am not going to copy off anybody to try and get in top group', Y9). Some respond with anger, as Boaler *et al.*'s data demonstrates:

> Obviously we're not the cleverest, we're group 5, but still – it's still maths, we're still in Year 9, we've still got to learn. (p. 646)

For others, being in the low set comes to be seen as their allotted station in school life – it is like a prison sentence that they can do little about. Some show a passive resignation while others respond by playing it tough, indicating that they are in control and have *chosen* to be there. As a result, they manage to blur the line between academic capability and behaviour as a basis for allocation to sets. Other pupils respond differently and explain the humiliation of wearing the bottom set label:

> It just makes you feel smaller than everybody else because you're in a lower set than all your friends. (Y8)

> Well I'm in the bottom group now and I feel horrible because people are saying that you are dumb and things like that. (Y9)

The lower sets are for 'the bad people' or for the people who are 'rubbish'. As Covington (1992) says: 'It is not surprising that the pupil's sense of esteem often becomes equated with ability – to be able is to be valued as a human being but to do poorly is evidence of inability, and reason to despair of one's worth' (in Chaplain, 1996, p. 102).

The comments so far have come mainly from pupils who do not make it to the top groups but others support setting because they see top groups as offering a sanctuary where they can get on with their work without disturbance from those who mess about – 'constant singing in class, swearing, throwing things, shouting' – and who consequently lure the teacher from *teaching* the class to *controlling* the class. And if poor behaviour is not the main problem, some pupils complain that the teacher goes too slowly for them in an attempt to make sure that 'the other' pupils can keep up.

What matters here is to find ways, *in mixed-ability grouping*, of ensuring and sustaining a steady concentration on the task and in *same-ability grouping* to remove the stigma and self-doubt that attaches to those in the lower groups. The widespread investment in individualized profiling and the discussion of different learning styles is helping to legitimize alternative ways of approaching tasks and minimizing the blanket labelling that some of the pupils quoted above have clearly suffered from. As work on profiles increases and as pupils accept that most of their peers will have, in their profiles, a mix of highs and lows for different subjects or skills, then grouping may seem more logical. But if the dominant impulse behind grouping practices is to separate the wheat from the chaff, as the Finnish boy said, then a lot of pupils will continue to feel justifiably aggrieved.

Tests and grades

In the last section we focused on the way that grouping practices influence the construction of self; here we discuss the influence of tests – recalling that the amount of testing that young people today are subjected to in school is greater than it has ever been. We have already seen how Year 8 pupils typically describe the character of Years 8 to 11: 'Y8 is getting ready for your SATS, Y9 is going through your SATs, Y10 is starting your GCSEs, Y11 is finishing your GCSEs' (m, Y8): clearly, for pupils, schooling is about tests and exams.

It is important to consider whether, as a result of the increase in dividing practices in school – such as grouping and testing – we are giving messages to some young people early in their school careers that make them think they are failures because they are not good enough at the narrow band of 'things that matter to schools', however good they might be at other things. In a powerful article, Reay and Ball (1999) wrote about a primary school pupil who said this in interview:

> I'm really scared about the SATs ... I'm no good at spelling and [our] class teacher is giving us times tables tests every morning and I'm hopeless at times tables so I'm frightened I'll do the SATs and I'll be a nothing. (1999, p. 345)

The researchers explained that this pupil was 'an accomplished writer, a gifted dancer and artist and good at problem solving' but she had a view that academic success is about correct spelling and knowing your tables and so she 'constructs herself as a failure, an academic non-person' by a shift 'in which she comes to see herself entirely in terms of the level to which her performance in the SATs is ascribed' *(ibid,* p. 346). The teacher is reported as having said to the whole class, 'I want to say that you are judged at the end of the day by what you get in the SATs and some of you won't ever get Level 2'. Another pupil, in the same class, said that if Level 2 was all she was going to get then she 'might not have a good life in front of me and I might grow up and do something naughty or something like that' *(ibid.).*

These are not isolated examples; extracts from our own recent interviews with Year 3 students reveal the anxiety about self that, for some students, shadows the tests:

> Well, I'm sort of worried in tests because you get a mark and if it's not that good ... We had this test and I was afraid I would get really low down. (Y3, m; in Doddington *et al.,* 2001, p. 28)

As Doddington *et al.* say in their report on Year 2 to Year 3 transition: 'It is not only pupils with lower levels of attainment who expressed negative feelings about tests. Some pupils were concerned because tests were presented in a way which emphasised what they could *not* do rather than what they could do' (2001, p. 29).

Although we are primarily interested here in the impact of tests on pupils' images of self as learner, the levels of general anxiety that they create must affect pupils' confidence and also their perception of learning. A Year 3 girl said, 'I don't really like doing tests because you're thinking, "Oh, what's this? What's this?" And you're really like sweating and everything' *(ibid.,* p. 28). There is no doubt that for some teachers tests and exams are the markers of what is important and this attitude is effectively communicated to pupils and to parents: 'Teachers give you the impression in class that GCSEs are the most important thing you'll ever do in your whole life' (Y11, f) and one parent was reported to have told her child that once the Year 2 SATs were over, he need not worry again until Year 6 (Doddington *et al.,* 2001). Learning to learn is in danger of becoming less important than doing well in the tests – and tests are not necessarily supportive of authentic learning.

Of course, there are many pupils who like tests, for both good and bad reasons: some say they like the spirit of competition, others like tests because they give structure and point to the school week or school term, or because they serve to break learning down into less daunting 'chunks'. Some like having a regular check on progress and say that getting things wrong shows where you have to work harder and is a means of getting 'lots of help' from the teacher. Other pupils, however, see tests as an investigative and controlling device that allows the teacher to check out whether 'you've been listening' and 'know more than you used to'. There is also evidence of a functional link in pupils' minds between test outcomes and grouping:

> I think (testing) is for the teacher to see how well you are actually doing in the class and to put you into different grades. (Y3, m; in Doddington *et al.*, 2001, p. 29)

> Tests are probably because teachers want to see how good we are and probably put us on a higher table. (Y3, m; *ibid.*)

These comments, however, were not emotionally charged – pupils were merely reporting the way things are. But, as Reay and Ball have said, the non-emotional tone – and the silences – are what allow us to think, conveniently, that either the 'national curriculum assessments have minimal impact on children's subjectivities or that children's concerns and attitudes are merely a backdrop to the assessment process, simply part of the social context' (1999, p. 346). Indeed, the Assessment Reform Group reminded its readers (1999, p. 5) of 'the profound influence' assessment can have 'on the motivation and self-esteem of pupils, both of which are crucial influences on learning'. It is this group which has led an important shift in perception from 'assessment *of* learning' to assessment *for* learning', thereby minimizing some of the negative effects of a competitive sorting process.

Selecting (or being selected by) your secondary school*

Feelings of lack of self-worth are not just related to being in a low set or doing badly in tests. Another critical experience is transfer to secondary school – and here the problem stems from the task of choosing a secondary school or, as some experience it, being chosen *by* a secondary school.

---

* Note: the quotations in this section are, unless otherwise referenced, from Isobel Urquhart's project; some but not all appear in Urquhart, 2001 and Rudduck and Urquhart, in press.

Isobel Urquhart opens an article (2001) with the following extract from a newspaper:

> It's two days since 11-year-old Frances heard she'd got into the secondary school she was hoping for, and she's still walking on air. (*Guardian Education*, 20 March 2001)

She comments: 'By celebrating the successes of those individuals who achieve places at popular and high achieving schools, press reports often draw readers' attention to the emotional highs of choosing a secondary school. And yet, for many children, the experience of choosing a school is one of protracted anxiety and ultimate disappointment' (p. 83).

Earlier research on transfer moved through several phases: in the 1960s and 1970s, before consumer choice in the context of market forces became a big issue, research tended to focus on the anxieties attendant on the move to the big school – not just the rite of passage stories about having your head put down the toilets but also ordinary, everyday concerns about travelling to a school which might be further away from home, finding your way around a larger school, getting used to new teachers and new ways of doing things and being able to cope with the work. Later, as the principle of choice was affirmed by governments, so a new set of studies appeared which focused on the determinants of choice of school and the relative power of pupils and parents in the decision-making process (David *et al.*, 1997; Reay and Ball, 1998). Lucey and Reay (1999) extended the research agenda by focusing on the impact on pupils of not getting their first choice of school, and Urquhart, in a study commissioned by one local education authority, replicated the research on a smaller scale.

Both studies gathered data from pupils in multi-ethnic inner-city schools in socially disadvantaged areas and both were undertaken 'against the backdrop of a pervasive rhetoric of "freedom to choose" [which is silent about the] growing evidence that increasing numbers of children . . . are being refused places at the school of their choice' (Wolchover, 1998; in Lucey and Reay, 1999, p. 5). Urquhart quotes one pupil she interviewed who said, 'Well I don't think it's fair really because my cousin, yeah, she got ten choices [of her secondary school] and all ten she failed. She's like me. I feel like an orphan' (Y6, f). Urquhart's study echoes a concluding statement in Lucey and

Reay's paper: 'These children's voices reveal just how traumatising and demoralising the business of choosing a school can be for those who fail to be selected by their first choice of school.' Indeed, as Urquhart says, 'The emotional turbulence runs much deeper than popular accounts suggest' (p. 83).

This early experience of being rejected by the secondary schools they'd chosen – at a time when they were enthusiastic about 'getting a good education' – was difficult for pupils to cope with:

> I was a bit sad when I got the letter – my mum didn't want to show it to me ... I just thought I weren't that good at things really. (Y6, f)

> I think people do sometimes get upset when they think they're the only one who haven't got in and they start to think they're not smart or they've done something wrong. (Y6, f)

> Why did they pick them not me? ... You think you must be bad. (Y6, f)

A few, however, vented their anger on the shortcomings of the process; their logic is persuasive – and their commitment to learning is poignantly impressive:

> I done a test and my head was aching ... and I don't care if it hurts my head ... the more education I get the more I'll learn ... They should take the ones who haven't (got) more education – they need more. (Y6, m)

> I didn't really like choosing schools ... they shouldn't be able to make you do tests because they're just looking at answers and it's not going to tell you much about *you*, is it, so I would say interviews are best; tests [only] tell you about what work they can do and how smart they are. (Y6, m)

Some students, in an effort at self-protection, claimed not to mind but the hurt was apparent:

> It kind of makes my work go down because it's like, because ... I don't really care because I've only got a school that's rubbish, I don't really care. (Y6, m)

Others rationalized their rejection in a variety of ways:

> I probably didn't get in because I don't go to church – it's a church school isn't it? I don't go to church often. (Y6, f)

All the schools do the same work really so it doesn't really matter what school you go to because you just do the same thing there whatever school you go to. (Y6, f)

I know why [school] rejected me – we had to take a test but they never wrote down my test scores, they just said there were two hundred or something girls there so they didn't take me. They never wrote down my test scores – I don't know why. (Y6, f)

A few years ago students' self-esteem within the peer culture was related to the make of their trainers; now, within these groups of students, the currency is whether or not you've got a place in a 'good' secondary school – and sometimes, as students acknowledged in the interviews, they will lie to others about which school they are going to in order to save face. Lucey and Reay (1999) made the interesting point that there emerged among the 'successful' 'a group identity based on a reassuring consensus that they had chosen and been chosen by the "best" schools'.

What we are arguing here is that if students feel rejected by the system early in their career as learners – and the hope is that that career will continue beyond school – then they will be wary about chancing their luck in situations where they think they might fail and will opt instead for withdrawal or a minimum effort – minimum risk – minimum achievement strategy. As Lucey and Reay commented – and their analysis is confirmed by Urquhart's study – 'a significant number of working class children conveyed the sense that they were on the brink of an event (transfer to the secondary school) which would have identity implications for them far into the future'.

Changing your image as learner

The dividing practices that prevail in schools today have the potential, not surprisingly, to create groups of pupils who have poor self-images in relation to the school's main purpose of learning. We know about the labels that researchers have coined to summarize patterns of behaviour within different pupil groups but we are concerned not so much with the labels attached by researchers but more with how pupils see themselves, and how they are seen by their peers and teachers. We are also interested in how tensions and pressures can lead pupils to adopt particular personas in school and classroom and with the difficulties they have in adapting or dropping them.

Negative images, once established in the individual pupil's behaviour patterns, are difficult to throw off: 'It's all right saying "Change"; but you can't just stop like that, can you?' (Y10, m, in Galton *et al.*, 2003). Another student, who seemed to have adopted an anti-boff identity as a way of avoiding tasks which he knew he was not good at, acknowledged that messing about had become 'addictive'. And students who have become the class joker find it particularly difficult to change because their peers have certain expectations of them – as this young woman explained:

> I think trouble with me were when I come to school I messed about from day one so people got me as a mess-abouter from day one so like if I didn't mess about, 'Oh, you're boring'. You know what I mean? (Y11, f; in Rudduck, 1998, p. 140)

But when it gets to exam time in Years 10 and 11 the old magic no longer works: instead of being the hero/clown they may find themselves rejected by the mates they once entertained. In such a situation, students may find it easier to give up than to try to change direction and catch up with their work. Students can also feel that their image and habits are held in place by their teachers – who have files and memories in which their behaviours and indeed their characters are indelibly recorded:

> ... you mess around ... you get a reputation for yourself as a trouble causer and you can't lose it – it's like there. (Y11, m; in Rudduck, 1998, p. 140)

Students understand what is at stake and are often surprisingly insightful and tolerant – take this 'difficult' Year 10 student, for instance:

> Me personally I've brought a reputation upon myself. I'm known to be the class clown and that and it's got me in a lot of trouble. And so I've decided to change and it's just really hard to, like show the teachers that 'cos ... and then, like, I went on report, and I got, like, A1, A1, best, top marks. But there's been some lessons where it's slipped and they're [saying] like, 'Oh, he's still the same'. I can understand how they feel about that. (Y10, m, in Rudduck, 1998, p. 139)

It is not surprising that students like teachers who believe in 'a fresh start'. One spoke with warmth of a teacher who starts the session by reminding the class that while their learning needs to be carried forward, each lesson is a clean slate as far as their behaviour is concerned.

In the past, a common resort of the desperate teacher or school has been to transfer a difficult student to another form or another school but those who have experienced such transfer say that students in the new setting know that comers-in are 'baddies' and so their reputation travels with them. The irony is that many of these students – like the students who failed to get a place in their preferred secondary school – *want* to learn and to do well. A Year 10 student speaks for a lot of students who find learning in school a struggle:

> I'll be honest, because I'm not exactly a very hard-working student, but when it comes down to it I also want to do well in my exams. (Y10, m)

In interviews conducted a few weeks before the start of the 16+ exams there were a lot of regrets from the pupils who had been, for whatever reasons, laid back about work and/or who had regularly sought to disrupt the work of their classmates. Interestingly, pupils mostly directed the blame to themselves even though in our view the system had often created the conditions in the first place which led to a non-work persona being adopted. They also tended to see the situation as irredeemable:

> I were just running about like a little kid and not doing owt. I was really immature ... and then it were like [this year] it hit me ... I could have tried harder but can't turn back time. (Y11, f)

> I missed loads of school which was my own fault and I'm suffering from that now ... I thought oh it doesn't matter I can make up the work but I didn't. I don't know what we're doing so it's a waste of time now. (Y11, m)

> When I think back I would have liked you know to start again because I realize now that there's been so much time that we've just wasted. Like we say to each other, 'Better start working' – something trivial would always crop up and that would be our main priority ... The fifth

year seemed years away and [I thought] that we'd be like so mature by then and we'd naturally have all As and that. But it didn't happen that way. [We had a note from Year 11s saying] 'You won't realize how much you need your education'. [But] what's a note to us? It's just, oh, read it and throw it away. All we wanted to do was play about. But if there's some way of showing them how instead of progressing some people do regress in subjects ... I don't know how that could be done. (Y11, m; in Rudduck, 1998, p. 139)

Pupils who see no possibility of changing and making good may well decide to opt out of the struggle: 'There's a few in our form that's settled down in the past year, that's got stuck into their work, but other people just don't care or don't bother coming to school' (Y10, f). Coping is difficult for those pupils whose self-confidence as learners and whose capacity to organize their lives effectively is fragile.

Sadly, we see more young people resolving the tension surrounding their own progress and status in school by construing the situation as one in which they are 'in a good place but unable to succeed' (Stevenson and Ellsworth, 1993, p. 266) – an experience which is easily transformed into what may be a lifelong perception that they are just 'not the right kind of person'. Such construction of self may affect individual pupils but it can also lead to groups of students becoming what Chaplain (1996, p. 109) called 'collaboratively disengaged' and who take heart in maintaining a noisy and extrovert disdain for school work. Members of such groups do not find it easy to escape the peer mores; indeed, we have had examples of pupils who wanted, but did not dare, to get on with their school work ask to be put on report so that they could blame their new commitment to learning on teachers' enforcement of the rules; sadly, this is usually only a short-term escape and once off report the student is likely to be recaptured by the group.

The starting point for some recent work with schools (see Galton *et al.*, 2003) was evidence of the difficulty pupils have in changing their image and attitude as learners. In the students' words it was about moving from being a 'dosser' or a 'shirker' to a 'worker', but these terms can give the impression that the problem is simply laziness and that the remedy lies exclusively in the students' hands. We think that this is only part of the story; there are often things within the regimes of schooling that make the students avoid work, and that can be remedied once teachers understand what they are.

The seven participating schools first identified the 'disengaged' students that they were most troubled about. The next step was to find a way of talking with them about the reasons for their disengagement. Some students, of course, are reluctant to open up to someone in the school but may do so with an outsider – whether youth worker or researcher – or in a group discussion. The data might reveal problems with pedagogy, problems in falling behind and the difficulty of catching up, problems in lack of responsibility or opportunities to take initiative compared with their lives outside school, a feeling that they are not valued highly by the school, and so on. Individually, they may acknowledge that they are part of a group that maintains a collective 'it's not cool to work' attitude and they may feel unable to, or frightened of, taking a different line.

Having identified the students who were in need of help and found out from them what they thought the source of their disengagement was, it was then time to consider the circumstances that might trigger change and to plan interventions. For some, the process of consultation may in itself be a turning point, helping students rid themselves of the feeling that 'they don't listen to us'. For others, it is moving into what they see as an important year and 'important years' tend to be the years with major tests or examinations. At these moments, some students will manage to change their own behaviours because they realize the time has come when learning needs to be taken seriously. For others, reassurance about their own capability is what can provide the trigger for change: as one said, 'SATs proved to me I could do it'; others may be able to build a new confidence in themselves by being asked to take on a special role or responsibility, or by being able to use, in the classroom, skills and talents developed outside school that do not usually find a place in the routine curriculum. (For instance one student gained self-respect and the respect of others by being given space to run a lunch-hour workshop on electronic design for his peers.) The process of disengagement can be reversed if students feel that significant others in the school are able to see and acknowledge some of their strengths.

The next stage was to plan an intervention that would fit the context and the needs of the students (here, we summarize the range of strategies that schools tried out):

- Some schools relied on regular conversations with youth workers as a way of supporting students in their 'retracking' – so that the target students knew that someone was always there for them.
- Some schools found it worked when disengaged students were invited to *choose* a teacher to be their mentor. This is an extra load for teachers but some say they find it more acceptable knowing that they have been 'chosen'. The teacher and the student have meetings – initially on a regular basis and later, when trust is established, as the student wants them – where problems with learning can be explored and worked through and manageable targets set so that students can build up a sense of progress and achievement.
- Some schools set up special units which provide space – a safe haven – for disengaged and/or disruptive students to cool down – somewhere they can get help talking through the problems they have with the routines of learning in school and guidance about catching up.

Legitimated peer support can also be valuable as students who are struggling will often respond more positively to peers who know they are having a difficult time but who do not use that knowledge to ridicule or humiliate them.

Other schools have tried an approach that tackles power networks within the peer group; the strategy is to identify leaders of anti-work groups and to support them in the task of exercising a benign pro-work influence on their followers. Such groups may be structured horizontally (i.e. the members are all in the same year cohort) or vertically (i.e. members are in different years but have something in common; in some settings the bond may be that the pupils belong to an out of school gang). Missionary roles are not generally popular with young people but an early demonstration, by teachers and by peers, of concern, support and respect for the leaders of such groups might help the leader to try to provide a more positive model for his or her followers.

While most teachers have an immediate concern, understandable in the present performance-oriented climate, with the very difficult task of bringing Year 10 students back on track so that they might make a better showing in the Year 11 examinations, they also recognize the advantage of identifying students at risk of disengaging in the earlier years when disaffection has not hardened into habit and when, consequently, 'rescue' attempts are less complex.

The teachers involved in the study were able to offer some cautionary advice on the basis of their experience:

- They suggested that whatever intervention or support is given it needs to be sustained over a period of time; one-off sessions are not enough.
- They told us that each new year cohort can develop a different character and bring a new raft of problems. Sources of disengagement may sometimes need to be examined in relation to the persona of the year group or its most difficult faction.
- They thought that more than one strategy might be needed to respond to the problems that lie behind the detached/dosser/clown attitudes that some pupils develop as a way of protecting themselves from negative learning experiences.

We can add some observations of our own:

- Schools may need to check out whether they are privileging some groups of students over others. They may be offering high-profile activities to some groups of students but not to all and if the disengaged are to come back on board they also need to feel that, as individuals, the school believes in them enough to offer them special support.
- Schools are familiar with mentoring schemes which give short-term intensive support, often to students who are on the borderline of a D/C grade at GCSE. Schemes which are highly selective and strategic may not always give priority to students who are struggling below the level which might make a real difference to the school's league table profile. Again, giving attention to these students can make them think that their learning matters.

- Moving the disruptive student to another group, class or school is at best a partial solution: disturbance to the work of peers is reduced but the target pupils' reputation travels with them and change of identity therefore remains difficult.

- Students see it as difficult to change their image if long-standing judgments held of them by teachers and by peers are not actively challenged. Both student and teacher need to feel, and assert, the opportunity to move on.

- Identities are held in place by the expectations, based on past behaviours, of both pupils and teachers; teachers who are open to 'fresh starts' – each day and each lesson – are respected by pupils who *want* to make the transition to 'worker'.

Mary Berry (in Galton *et al.*, 2003) produced a diagram (see Figure 1) to summarize possible starting points for teachers who want to support young people in changing their image and behaviours.

Figure 1

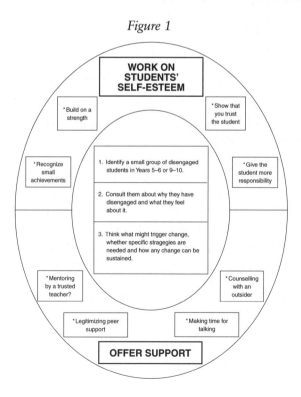

In concluding this section we want to point out that we have deliberately focused on things that are contributing to *poor* self-images among pupils and that leave a mark that is difficult to eradicate. We do so because in a climate of concern about progress we believe that some students may be under-achieving as a result of these negative self-images. Schools do not always provide a climate or occasions where young people can air their sense of injustice and talk about what they think the system is doing to them and we need to look out for the things that can damage their confidence and self-esteem, and encourage them to talk through their concerns. As Smyth and Hattam have said, 'in telling the stories of life, previously unheard or silenced voices open up the possibility for new, even radically different narrations of life experience' (2002, p. 378).

The Pedagogic Dimension

> One can alter curricula, change power relationships, raise standards ... but if these efforts are not powered by altered conceptions of what makes [students] tick and keeps them intellectually alive, willingly pursuing knowledge and growth, the results will be inconsequential. (Sarason, 1991, p. 163)

We know that pupils sometimes switch off in lessons because they are bored, or because they want to avoid work that is difficult, or because they are put off by noise in the classroom, or because they need individual help which the teacher is not able at that moment to give, or because the immediate task is less enthralling than thinking about or chatting about the intricacies of their social lives. These are the familiar day-to-day problems of teaching and learning, but if they are not responded to then pupils may come to accept them as part of the wearisome routinization of schooling and have difficulty in sustaining a genuine commitment to learning in school.

The strength of such commitment appears to depend on the fine tuning of challenge and engagement in the classroom, the reliability of school-wide frameworks of encouragement, respect and support, and on the potency of the peer group pro- and anti-work norms. And, of course, on the humanity and professional skill of the teacher. Pupils have talked to us about many aspects of teaching and learning in school – how the classroom environment affects learning, how they value feedback on their work rather than just grades, how very important it is for some of them to have good work recognized by their teachers and their parents. But here we are focusing on what students say about the two most accessible and predictable topics, 'What makes a good teacher' and 'What makes a good lesson'.

What makes a good teacher?

It is clear that the teacher is seen, by virtually all the students interviewed, as a key influence on learning: 'The teacher makes a lesson better, even if it's a lesson you hate ... a good teacher [can] make you like it.' But in the present judgmental climate teachers are, understandably, anxious lest consulting pupils means unlocking a barrage of criticism of them and their teaching. In our experience this is not usually the case: mostly pupils criticize the task or the procedures rather than the teacher and their commentaries are often very constructive. When we are talking to pupils in school settings we use a ground rule that no teacher is to be named – a rule which pupils respect – although one got round it by saying, 'There's a certain headteacher in this school who ...' However there are situations in which criticism is justifiable (see Chapter 6) and pupils do not always know how they can legitimately give voice, within the usual structures of schooling, to their concerns or anger. The research interview conducted by an outsider can provide the space that is missing in the usual routines of schooling. But the researcher then faces the problem of what can be disclosed; researchers know that pupils want something to happen but they will be properly cautious about the implications of their own agency.

Boaler and her colleagues encountered situations where pupils were looking for an occasion when they could explain their concerns. One, in a bottom set for maths, said that their group was the only one that 'kept changing teachers' and it was because 'they don't think they have to bother with us. I know that sounds really mean and unrealistic, but they just think they don't have to bother with us, 'cos we're group 5. They get, say, a teacher who knows nothing about maths, and they'll give them to us, a PE teacher or something. They think they can send anyone down to us. They always do that. They think they can give us anybody' (Boaler *et al.*, 2000, pp. 637–8). It is not surprising (see later) that respect and fairness feature so prominently in pupils' taxonomies of the qualities of a good teacher.

In settings where there is no bottling up of injustices and resentment we are often surprised by pupils' capacity for situational analysis and in particular for seeing things from the teacher's perspective. For instance, pupils interviewed by Pedder and McIntyre (2001) explained that their teacher persisted in repeating instructions – a habit which annoyed them – because she wanted to make sure that 'the slower ones' had understood the task; this was a concern they sympathized with but they suggested, eminently sensibly, that she repeat it to 'the slower ones' separately because whole-class repetition was slowing the others down.

What pupils say about good teachers is rooted in experience; it has the familiar comfort of common sense and this may be why some aspects of their analysis are given less serious attention in improving learning than they deserve: familiarity doesn't guarantee that they are carefully monitored at the level of whole-school practice.

Our original summary of the qualities of a good teacher was based on a series of interviews with secondary school pupils in three schools in the north of England (see Rudduck, Day and Wallace, 1996a, p. 86). We went on to ask similar questions of pupils in other schools in different parts of the country – including 10 schools participating in our *Learning About Improvement Project* in West Sussex. There was remarkable consistency across pupils in the different schools. We decided to produce a composite list, from the data gathered in different projects, and to allocate the items to four broad sets of 'qualities'. Good teachers are (the order is not significant):

- human, accessible and reliable/consistent;
- respectful of students and sensitive to their difficulties in learning;
- enthusiastic and positive;
- professionally skilled and expert in their subject.

We can fill out each of these broad topics, using, as far as possible, the words of the pupils.

Good teachers are human, accessible, reliable and consistent
- They are fair
- They are people you can talk to
- They don't give up on you
- They don't just remember the bad things you have done
- They are consistent in their mood
- They are calm and have a sense of humour
- They understand students and treat them 'like an equal'
- They know what it is like to be young and a teenager
- They have common sense
- They are not petty over silly things
- They don't take things personally
- They can admit they have made a mistake.

Good teachers are respectful of students and sensitive to their difficulties
- They don't go on about things (like how much better other classes are or how much better your older brothers and sisters are)
- They don't shout
- They don't make fun of you or humiliate you in front of others
- They are not sarcastic or vindictive
- They do not speak to you in an irritating tone of voice
- They don't assume students have not listened when help is asked for
- They respect students so that students can respect teachers
- They will let pupils have a say and will listen to them
- They explain things and will go through things you don't understand without making you feel small
- They believe students when students tell them something
- They treat students as individuals rather than just one of the mass.

Good teachers are enthusiastic and positive
- They enjoy being a teacher
- They enjoy teaching the subject
- They enjoy teaching us
- They give praise more than punishment
- They make you think you can do well
- They don't put red lines all through things you've worked hard on
- They don't say, 'I would rather not be teaching you'
- They don't say 'You're the worst class I have ever taught'.

Good teachers are professionally skilled
- They make the lesson interesting and link it to life outside the school
- They will have a laugh but know how to keep order
- They are knowledgeable in their subject but know how to explain
- They find out who needs help and give it
- They vary the way they teach to suit the students in their classes
- They allow some input from the students
- They find ways of giving students choices.

What struck us was that the qualities that matter to pupils tend to be as much about how they are *treated* as how they are *taught*. Having a good relationship with teachers can be an important element in pupils' commitment to learning and may also help them to resist being captured by the 'school work isn't cool' lobby. A positive discovery in one school in another LEA was that the majority of the 19 under-achieving boys consulted through a questionnaire said that they would like more opportunity to talk with teachers about their school work – although they would prefer to do so in ways that would not involve them in losing face in front of their peers. If there were more time for dialogue about school work so that it became a regular feature of school life, then pupils might be less embarrassed about being seen talking about their learning.

Interestingly, teachers who embody the virtues listed above are not, it would seem, hard to find. Students were abstracting the qualities they appreciated from their daily experience of lessons with a variety of clearly excellent and trusted teachers across a range of subjects. The issue was how to extend these 'good' qualities – which the students were very perceptive about – within their schools.

What makes a good lesson?
What was striking about pupils' views of the qualities of a good teacher was the consistency across schools. A similar consistency appears in pupils' judgments of what makes a good lesson. Here, as above, we have grouped the items from the interview data from various projects under four broad headings. Most pupils respond well to:

- opportunities for participation and engagement;
- active lessons with a variety of learning tasks;
- challenge (that is exciting but not overwhelming); and
- opportunities to exercise autonomy.

These topics are, again, so familiar they don't readily hook into our consciousness and don't therefore get onto our school improvement agenda. We may therefore underestimate their *cumulative* effect on motivation across different subjects and over time. We shall discuss each of them briefly, with illustrations from pupil commentaries and, where possible, give attention to their less predictable margins.

Good lessons are about participation and engagement
Being able to participate is, for pupils, almost synonymous with being engaged. The widespread support for participation links into issues of ownership and intellectual excitement but it is also about understanding, and thereby having some control over, the nature and purpose of the task. Participation is more than just answering questions in a quiz – although pupils often ask for games that are fun *and* educational. It can be about working in groups or pairs on a task that pupils understand and feel motivated to work on; such tasks may find their starting point in pupils' curiosities, they may involve finding things out from sources outside the classroom or designing solutions to problems that matter. But it can also be about a form

of instructional teaching that helps pupils feel, as a class, a sense of collective purpose and excitement.

This is how pupils talk about participation and engagement:

> I like it when everyone joins in and it's not just the teacher talking and pupils listening, like when the whole class gets involved and everyone's like giving their point of view.

> Sharing ideas amongst the class helps you to feel more involved in the subject.

> The thing that I liked was that the whole class got up and participated in the activity.

> I like working in groups. It gives me confidence.

(Nick Brown, fieldwork data)

There's also an awareness among pupils of the way that exam pressures can constrain the kind of lesson where they think they work well: 'In [Subject X] it's rush, rush, rush. There's never enough time to have a discussion. [So you don't get] other people's points of view . . . [which] makes me understand more.'

Good lessons include activity and variety

At some level the secondary school day offers its own kind of variety: pupils move from classroom to classroom, subject to subject and teacher to teacher in ways that provide change but not always the satisfaction of being able to go into depth or finish something you are really interested. And even within the span of 40 minutes or an hour, pupils can become restless. We know that they don't like 'listening to the teacher going on and on' or copying from board or book for long stretches of time, and attention spans may be influenced by the practice in action-packed TV narratives of running several themes simultaneously and constantly shifting from one to the other. Boys in particular often tell us that they want to be able to move around in lessons and neither boys nor girls look forward to lessons where 'what you do is always the same, week after week':

> I think in some subjects there's a lot of variety and you can do a lot of different things and it's really good and the teaching is very ... very ... a high standard. But with others, it's terrible ... it's the same thing

every lesson and you just want to, like, kill someone and it's just …
God! … yeah, it's awful. (Nick Brown, fieldwork data)

A classic comment on such wasteful boredom in lessons comes from
a much earlier study of learning in the sixth form (Rudduck and
Hopkins, 1984, p. 25):

> He'll read out of the book, mumble, mumble, mumble, and it is all
> you can do to keep awake . . . and you can see others making paper
> aeroplanes – a sixth former making paper aeroplanes! You just can't
> read a whole section out of a book like that!

Other students express similar irritation, although in less extreme
ways:

> I like lessons when we have to do something [not just] read, write and
> listen – things that gets your hands on and doing stuff, [where] you
> have to use your brain.

> You need writing but you also need to be active sometimes.

> Copying is a bit boring 'cos you don't get to do your own work.

On the other hand, when they are genuinely engaged pupils will
spend a lot of time on a task, and when they can use computers
they may be more tolerant of tasks that involve writing. The issue
of 'variety and activity' may, therefore, be task related as well as, to
some degree, gender related.

Good lessons are ones which challenge you and make you think
Some students want to avoid challenge at all costs because they fear
they may not be up to it or because challenge requires upping their
usual level of commitment. Other students want to be challenged
because challenge stimulates you, makes you think and therefore
helps you to learn. Some students like the comfort of Year 7 or Year 8
being a repetition of last year's work because they know they can do
it, while others want to move on and learn more. Some are angry that
they are not being stretched and enabled to learn properly, especially
if they are in a low set in a school where upper sets seem to them
to be privileged. As one student poignantly remarked: 'Obviously
we're not the cleverest, we're group 5, but still – it's still maths, we're

still in Year 9, we've still got to learn' (Boaler *et al.*, 2000, p. 646). Others dislike short cuts to learning – where getting things right matters more than understanding what you are doing, or where 'safe' consolidation is valued more than 'risky' original work:

> He gave 9×9 to me and I said, '81'. And he goes to somebody else, 'What's 7 times?' – or someat like that. And they said someat really stupid like 59. And do you know what he did? He didn't go, 'Oh, well, you are meant to do it like this', he just gave them a sheet and said, 'Every time you need to, look it up on the sheet'. (Y8, m; Harris, fieldwork data)

> In history I've got half my books filled with answers to questions and then they say, 'Do an essay on it' and all it is is writing it up again … We've already written it three times! I think that is a waste of time. 'Oh, excellent essay' [they say]. It is just answers to the questions and even [those were copied up] from the sheet so it is not really your own work. (Y11, m; Harris, fieldwork data)

Another student, from Boaler *et al.*'s research, is uneasy about the assumed link between copying and learning and about the lack of intellectual challenge in copying:

> Once or twice someone has said something and he's shouted at us, he's said, 'Well, you're in the bottom group, you've got to learn it'. But you're not going to learn from copying off the board. (2000, p. 638)

These young students are making a justifiable distinction between 'proper' learning, where things go into your brain, and short-cut learning, where things move straight from the board or the text into your notebook, by-passing your brain. Like other socially disadvantaged students they want to do well but don't always understand how that translates into the minutiae of everyday practice:

> Yeah, well you have to work really hard but it's all worth it really. Yeah, 'cos you're going to get a good education later on, if you like. If you don't want a good education then there's no point in coming to school. (Y6, m; in Rudduck and Urquhart, in press).

> I done a test … that was quite long and my head was aching but at least I know what I'm doing and I don't care if it hurts my head …

the more education I get the more I'll learn – so that's what I need. (Y6, m; in Rudduck and Urquhart, in press).

Such pupils deserve sustained challenge and support.

Good lessons are ones which offer students some autonomy
Some years back a sixth form teacher wrote this (Fox, in Rudduck, 1991, p. 43):

> I think my greatest annual moment of depression is the arrival of a new sixth form fresh from their [exam] triumph. 'Sir, Sir, our mouths are open: shovel in The Truth and we'll regurgitate it in the A level.' The external examinations, I feel, can trap a teacher and a class mercilessly. If I could, I would ask the sixth form to determine its own course to a very great extent; groups or individuals would make contracts with the teacher to tackle pieces of work, devised in consultation with the teacher – not too closely preplanned, to allow room for expansion and alteration as the directions of the group are discovered. The teacher is not an authority figure – but a human centre of information and assistance.

Autonomy is identified by many researchers (see Anderman and Maehr's review, 1994) as a key factor in pupils' commitment to learning in school. But for researchers, as well as for pupils, the term has many shades of meaning. The last quotation illustrates a *teacher*'s frustration at the continuing dependence and caution of his students as they enter the sixth form. But again and again in interviews we hear *students*' pleas for more 'autonomy' – by which they seem to mean more opportunity to make decisions about what they do in class, tasks where they can 'work things out for themselves' or learn from each other, and (as we saw earlier) learning that they have actively constructed rather than just copied into a notebook. Among older students, 'autonomy' may also be a shorthand for wanting to be seen as, and to be able to act as, an individual rather than as one of a group. A clutch of quotations from different projects and from pupils of different ages will give some sense of the range of meanings:

> I like lessons ... when I am given freedom in my work.

> I like it when the whole class is involved. It's more like teaching each other than the teacher just teaching us.

I enjoyed this lesson as we worked in partners and didn't have to have any help from the teacher.

I like to be set tasks with some variation or element that I control.

I like learning [when] I'm learning for me, for when I leave school. I'm not learning for being in school. It's to be successful. I personally like independent learning, like me going off and finding out stuff for myself.

In the passage quoted earlier, Fox was concerned to free his sixth form students from blind dependence on him as organizer of their learning. Gill Mullis recently described how it had taken her two years to train her students (now in Y11) to feel confident about planning with her how to make the most of their lessons together:

I've had these situations in class now where I've said, 'Laura, could you do this bit [of the lesson] – could you scribe at the top? Reena, could you do the OHT?' And I've actually handed far more over to them in lessons than I would have done a year ago. I hear myself saying, 'Right, this is what we need to learn in the next nine weeks, this is what you need to revise, these are the number of sessions – what do you think we need to do first? What do we do next?' You know, far more consultation. (Mullis, 2002, p. 3)

But Fox was also concerned about the pupils seeing him as the expert. Most students are not in a position to question the teacher's authority. And the pedagogy does not usually encourage them to seek evidence that might demonstrate the complexity of competing claims to knowledge. Of course, a 'good' teacher is likely to encompass this in his or her teaching, revealing the structure of alternatives that lie behind a synthesis, but there are many students for whom knowledge is what lies between the covers of the textbook, exists in the teacher's mind, or is on the computer screen. The sixth form has traditionally been the place where students are expected to start to think for themselves but even here the spectre of the examination can force students back onto accepting the teacher's statements as a proper representation of meaning and the teacher's questions rather than their own as guides to the proper routes of enquiry. Indeed, as one student pointed out in interview, using a strikingly persuasive image, autonomy at sixth form is like being let loose on a slightly longer lead. And as Ian Frowe observes, '... the need to "get on" has infected the whole educational experience so that there is little or no time for genuinely open conversations through which children may have opportunities to develop their understanding and learning' (Frowe, 2001, p. 98).

Some students manage to break away earlier – perhaps because their teachers help them – and enjoy a fledgling independence of thought. They are learning to accept that their teacher is no longer claiming certainty and cannot therefore be relied on to go on holding out an intellectual safety net for them. They see that students must begin to take responsibility for their own intellectual performances:

> In the sixth form, even if what they say is 'right', you have got to stand back from what they say and ask: 'Are they totally right about that?' and not just write it down as they say it and not think about it.

> You've always got to be having in your head the word 'bias'. I mean whatever information you are given, whether you read it or you are told, I have often the tendency to take that as fact ... I mean the whole idea of A level, not necessarily A level, the whole idea of higher education is to question it for yourself and therefore get more out of it for yourself. (Rudduck and Hopkins, 1984, pp. 26–7)

These students are beginning to appreciate the play of their own minds; they see that reproducing the idea picked up from the book or the teacher 'is not nearly as much fun as developing your own [ideas] and trying them out'.

Teaching for intellectual growth and teaching for examination passes are not necessarily the same and it is not easy in the present climate for teachers to avoid some degree of sacrifice of the one to the other. And with national targets for increased access to higher education and a possible upward drift in grades, teachers may see their contract with students in terms of ensuring the achievement of good examination passes as the passport to continued study. The point at which it is expected that students will think for themselves, perhaps the key dimension of autonomy, may also be on an upward drift – deferred until they get to college or university.

*

It would be useful if schools were able to review the reasonableness of pupils' comments on teachers and teaching and monitor practice across lessons to check out whether, for a good deal of each day and week, approaches reflect what pupils would identify as 'good practice' in helping them learn.

At both primary and secondary level we were concerned by data that showed how repeated testing was hammering out, for some, a negative image of self as learner and a negative experience of learning as a source of stress. We were also concerned about the image of learning that was gradually building up through pupils' school careers. Learning comes to be experienced and construed as a series of intense, short-term bursts for the test or the exam. The term the 'quick fix' has become part of the discourse of school improvement but in these conditions learning itself has the characteristics of a quick fix. Primary teachers argued, in recent interviews in two LEAs, that the focused work for the Key Stage 1 tests tuned the pupils to concert pitch – and that after the concert was over, they returned to their 'natural' pitch – hence the dip in progress in Year 3 (this was only one of several ways of explaining the dip, of course, but one that many Year 3 teachers in the project schools subscribed to; see Doddington *et al.*, 2001).

We know that we want all pupils to develop a positive sense of themselves as learners but what conception of learning do we want pupils to develop in school and what kind of learning do we want them to value if they are to move confidently and competently into learning beyond school? It is a sad moment when Year 11s are heard saying, 'Now the exams are over I never want to look at another book in my life'.

The Social Dimension

Interviwer: What do you look forward to at school – in the morning when you say 'Oh I want to go to school because . . .'?

Year 2 boy: I like seeing my friends when I come to school, and lining up.

(Rudduck, fieldwork data)

In this section we try to understand how pupils see the balance – and the links between – the social and academic arenas and opportunities of schooling. First we hear five- to six-year-olds talking about what matters to them in school; then we look at the way older pupils, faced with a tension between the social and the academic demands of their lives, sort out their priorities, and finally we go on to look at what pupils say about the links between friends and learning – and the implications of this for grouping practices, particularly in the year following transfer to the secondary school.

Lessons and breaktimes

As adults we may think of school in terms of classrooms, the curriculum, and teachers teaching but for pupils being at school is a social occasion as much as an opportunity for academic learning. Indeed, Blatchford's research underlines the importance for pupils of breaktimes – periods of the day when they are relatively 'freed from the attention of adults and the structure of the classroom' and can interact in their own ways, whether through games of their choosing or relationships of their making. It is a time

> when important social networks are formed; a time when pupils can fall out, but can also develop strategies for avoiding conflict. It is a time when pupils can find freedom and a social life independent of the classroom, where the rules of conduct are more their own, and where activities stem from their own initiative. (1998, p. 1)

In short, there is an alternative learning agenda outside the classroom, although pupils may not recognize these learnings and do not talk about them as such: learning how to initiative activities and work out rules for shaping the behaviours of participants in games, learning how to mediate in disputes, and so on. The value of these social learnings may also go relatively unnoticed by adults in the current climate of concern about performance and academic standards.

In our own small-scale study, six six-year-olds were asked what they liked or didn't like about school and their responses were invariably located in 'their' part of the school day rather than in lessons (the pupils were interviewed in pairs):

Interviewer: Can you think of anything exciting that you have done at school? It can be anything, it doesn't have to be now, it could be last year or anytime. Can you think of anything?

Girl 1: Play games with people.

Interviewer: Play games, outside or in the classroom or ...

Girl 1: Outside.

Interviewer: Is that at playtime?

Girl 1, Boy 1: Yeah.

Interviewer: What do you think are the most important things that you learn at school?

Boy 2: Fighting and kicking.

Interviewer: What did you say?

Boy 2: Fighting and ...

Interviewer: Fighting?

Boy 2: Yeah.

Interviewer: You think that is the most important thing that you learn at school [name]?

Boy 2: But I never hurt anybody.

Interviewer: Do you enjoy school?

Girl 2: Sometimes I don't and sometimes I do.

Interviewer: What about the don't times. Can you tell me when you don't enjoy it?

Girl 2: Because some of the people when they are playing football they get too excited and they, when they are running after the ball, they sort of like, just push me out the way.

(Rudduck, fieldwork data)

The responses are all the more surprising because the interviewer was the pupils' headteacher! It is clear that these pupils had not yet learnt to be strategic and were not giving 'please the teacher' responses by talking about learning in the classroom.

Not all pupils in Blatchford's study were positive about all aspects of breaktime. For example, the weather was mentioned as a source of frustration among younger pupils who presumably had nowhere else to go if it was raining; pupils also had concerns about anti-social behaviours in breaktimes.

Another, less predictable problem that emerged from our interviews was having nothing to do – a problem often associated with having no one to do anything with. Asked what they didn't like about school, some pupils, as though this was at the forefront of their concerns, talked about the problems of feeling lonely in the playground – which is after all an explicitly socially interactive situation – and the strategies they adopted to cope with the problem. It is interesting that boredom, in the first extract, is talked about not as something that happens in lessons but in the playground (again, the interviewer is the head teacher):

Interviewer: Are there times when you are bored at school?

Girl 1, Boy 1: [together] Yeah.

Boy 1: Yeah, sort of like when I got nobody to play with. I just sit in a corner, I do sometimes.

Interviewer: Are you sometimes bored at school?

Boy 3: Yes.

Boy 2: Sometimes I am bored because um … I don't want to, I don't want – it's cold out there and I don't want to play with anybody.

Interviewer: So that is out on the playground, is it? What do you do when you get bored, just sit on the bench or …

Boy 3: Normally I feel like, I feel like – I play games with my hands.

Interviewer: What about you [Boy 2], do you get bored at school?

Boy 2: Well um … when I get bored and don't have anybody to play with, I have got some toys inside my bag and I get them out and I just play with them.

Interviewer: Are you sometimes bored at school?

Girl 3: I get bored when um … no one is playing with me and um … I just have to walk around in the playground.

Interviewer: What do you do when you get bored?

Girl 3: Just walk around.

Interviewer: On your own?

Girl 3: Yeah.

Interviewer: What do you do [Boy 4] when you get bored?

Boy 4: Just sit on the bench and wait for somebody to come and ask who ever wants to play with me, and usually some people do. I get really bored and they come and say 'Do you want to play?' and I do.

(Rudduck, fieldwork data)

These five- to six-year-olds' desire for playmates, and the strategies they developed to compensate for or disguise their absence, suggested that they saw breaktimes outside the classroom as essentially occasions for positive social interaction; being without the means of interacting – i.e. not having friends – was clearly difficult for them to deal with.

It is interesting that the playground is one of the three clusters of social influence identified by Pollard and Filer (1996, p. 16) which 'can extend or constrain' the possibilities of formal learning: the first is *outside the school* – homes, parents and siblings; the second is *outside the classroom* – the school playground and the interactions among peers that take place there and the baggage that comes back into the classroom; the third, interaction with successive teachers and the judgments that they form of individual or groups of pupils, is *within the classroom*. However, we would single out *interaction with peers in the classroom* as a cluster of influence in its own right.

The expected allocation of territories is that in the playground social interaction is pupil-controlled and socially oriented whereas in the classroom social interaction is teacher controlled and learning-oriented – although we all know how skilled pupils are at winning control of segments of, and sometimes all of, the social interaction in the classroom. Reay and Arnot's work with Year 8 pupils in two secondary schools (2002) vividly shows how the pupils' interest in social interaction – and this is much more than just chatting to your friend – can be foregrounded in classrooms. They noted that pupils tend to 'describe classroom life through social interactions rather than subject knowledge ... The content of learning appears an irrelevance to their image of classroom life, except when it comes to comparison of their own abilities with those of others'. They found persuasive evidence of the often enthusiastic playing out of power differentials between different groups of students and they depict the classrooms in which pupils are expected to learn as 'full of fractious in-fighting, competing groups, and characterised by myriad bids for attention and status'. Their earlier paper (Arnot *et al.*, 2001) showed how the work-keen middle-class girls complained about the boys' deliberate strategies for slowing the pace of learning – and how, in turn, boys complained about how the girls 'zoom' and try to speed up the pace of teaching against the wishes of the boys. Different sub-groups within the same class *all* claimed that other groups were getting more attention than they were and contributed to a climate characterized by tensions, disruptions and resistances.

Inappropriate social interaction can be more easily dealt with if there are only one or two obvious culprits – although others may be willing audiences. However, where pupils experience it as tiresome and disturbing they can be sharply critical – although they may have no way of communicating their feelings directly to the teacher or of talking the issues through with the disrupters. Here, a Year 10 pupil comments sympathetically but firmly about the difficulties that the disrupters present to others:

> I mean there's always an individual in every group of people that disrupts lessons … and it's usual in most schools I'd have thought, but the problem is that there's more than one of these individuals. There are several. And they sort of encourage each other. And most of the teachers don't have the nerve to do something about it. They sort of back off. Those teachers that do try to do something about it, they just don't succeed because they're not backed up. Quite often the disruptive pupils get away with it … It's fine if it happens once every now and then – I'll be honest, because I'm not exactly a very hard-working student – but when it comes down to it, I do also want to do well in my exams. I'm not going to blame it all on disruptive pupils, but they do affect the lesson … I think everyone in the end, apart from the disruptive pupils, feels annoyed and unhappy about it because at the end of the day everyone wants to do well … The disruptive pupils, they're quite popular. They're nice people most of the time. But then it's almost as if school's too much for them. (Y10, m; Nick Brown's fieldwork data)

But another (Year 8) pupil's annoyance leads to a less temperate response:

> I get in arrears a lot you see . . . I don't look forward to going to [subject] because I know that it is like noisy in there. And sometimes when I want to be good, just because they are so noisy it does my head in, so I start shouting.

Primary pupils also talk to the visiting researcher about how noise gets in the way of their learning but without any strategy for dealing with it other than putting up with it:

> It's difficult to work when it's noisy in the classroom and I'm sitting down and everyone else is talking to one another. (Y3, m)

> I'd like to sit in a quiet corner of the classroom. (Y3, m)

We can see from these examples how very important the social world of school is for pupils and that it can be, at different times, a source of joy, pain and irritation.

Balancing school work and social activities

The tensions between the demands of young people's social lives and their commitment to school work sharpen around homework and revision, particularly as they move nearer to the Year 11 exams. Out of school, as in the playground, pupils have more control over how they use their time, and there are clear-cut choices to be made. Some pupils decide to give priority to school work whatever the social cost while others may decide to give priority to social concerns whatever the academic cost; a third group takes a middle way, developing a strategy that reflects what they consider to be the right balance for them of social and academic activities. This student manages the tensions through a disciplined segregation, with the scales tipped towards the social:

> Monday to Thursday . . . I do one and a half hours . . . On Fridays I do one hour . . . and then I don't do anything all day Saturdays or Sunday ... This routine means that my school work does not interfere at all with my private life. (Y11, m; in Rudduck *et al.*, 1996, p. 136)

The next student is also clear about what his priorities are and why he apportions time in this way:

> My school work fits into the gaps in my life, not the other way round. I figure that if I'm not enjoying my life I might as well be dead so I'll enjoy it as much as I can and school work is something to do in my spare time. (Y11, m; in Rudduck *et al.*, 1996, p. 136)

Whereas these two students seem in control of their decisions, other students whom we interviewed had no real control because their prioritization, both in school and outside, was determined by the culture of the groups or gangs they were members of. Reay and Arnot's data (2002) show how, in some contexts, 'cleverness marginalises you within the peer group' – although the hard-working and academically successful boys they describe were not unduly perturbed by being marginalized. In our own enquiries into friendship and learning (see Demetriou *et al.*, 2000) we discovered that individual students within anti-work peer groups who wanted to learn found it difficult to resist the pressure of the group and resorted to quite cunning strategies to maintain their position in the group while in fact giving attention to learning. One strategy, for instance, was to seek to be put 'on report' because then students could say to their mates that they were only working hard because the system of surveillance obliged them to. And in another study a Year 9 boy who was embarrassed at the idea of appearing eager to work or even to talk about school work suggested that schools needed 'them wooden things' that you get in churches – i.e. confessionals – where you could go in and discuss problems with your learning without your mates being able to see you and without the teacher knowing who it was. It is interesting that in this boy's peer culture, school work seemed to have acquired the trappings of sin.

Committing yourself to school work is not a straightforward undertaking for young people given that the period of schooling coincides with a changing and often turbulent set of experiences in their lives outside school; they are shaping and coming to terms with their social and sexual identities as well as their identities as learners and the three sets of interests are not always easy to manage.

What pupils say about sitting and working with friends*

Whenever the discussion touched on fantasy, fairness or friendship – 'the three Fs' I began to call them – participation zoomed upward. (Paley, 1986, p. 124)

The relationship between friendship, school work and achievement is not always straightforward. When young people start school and later move from primary to secondary school, friendships become prominent, particularly for parents who want to be sure that their children have a good friend – a source of social support – in the new setting. Blatchford's evidence (1998, p. 88) echoes this observation; he suggests that 'friendships can help reduce uncertainty and thus help adjustment to school'. More elusive is the link between friendships and academic progress and we have noted a tendency for teachers to be wary of friendships which they see as a potential source of distraction: 'Although they may be best buddies, when it comes to working in a classroom they just don't help each other because they are too ready to chat or mess about.' And they are right to be wary – but that is not the whole story.

Our data suggest that pupils are in fact very discerning when it comes to choosing their preferred working partners: they are able to judge which friends they work well with and which they don't work well with and under what circumstances. We concluded that it is often better to consult pupils about who they work well with rather than to impose seating patterns that they may find arbitrary and unproductive.

First, some comments from pupils who recognize that sitting with friends is not good for *them* and their work. Among a group of Year 10 students who had recently started on the work for the 16+ examinations were some who acknowledged that they lacked discipline. They wanted to work but knew that their concentration could quickly give way to social chat: if they were sitting with talkative friends they didn't feel able to break the social bond by

---

* Note: the pupil quotations in this section are, unless otherwise referenced, from the fieldwork conducted by Demetriou and Goalen for a project on transfer; reported in Galton *et al.*, 2003.

withdrawing and getting on with their work, and hoped the teacher would intervene and sort it out for them:

> Some friends . . . they don't like work as hard as other friends and it's quite hard just sort of telling them to work, because they're friends basically. (Y10, f)

> In my maths lesson I sat next to two of my friends, one was a girl and one was a boy, but my maths teacher moved me because we just always used to talk, they used to like distract me, so she moved me to sit by myself, which makes me work better. (Y10, m)

Another boy would also, it seems, given his 'warts and all' account of his friend's academic prowess, welcome being rescued by the teacher:

> He's one of my friends and he's a nice person but he doesn't have much of an attention span so whenever we are using water there's a problem because he'll be squirting water everywhere – we often get strange results. (Y10, m)

If in the earlier years of secondary schooling pupils had been able to take part in regular discussions of learning and the conditions of learning in the classroom, then it might be easier for them to talk together in Year 10, without fear of hurting each other, about the problems that they present for each other's learning.

A Year 8 pupil, also aware of his susceptibility, prefers to resist temptation by sitting apart – but the interesting thing about his comment is that he prioritizes those subjects that he wants to do well in:

> I prefer to work on my own. I can concentrate a lot better on my own sometimes. Depends what lesson it is. I want to do good in maths, it's one of my strong points and I find it easier to work on my own. (Y8, m)

Interestingly, some Year 3 pupils (in Flutter *et al.*, 1998) also made 'horses for courses' observations, distinguishing which tasks were better done on your own, and why:

> When I'm story writing I like to do it in the quiet with one sensible friend. Some people talk to you all the time. I like to be with someone who doesn't knock you, who's still and quiet. (Y3, f)

[With story writing I like to work] by myself. With friends you have to agree on a subject like fairies or adventures if you are working in a pair. (Y3, f)

We encountered a few pupils who were also reluctant to work with their peers, whether friends or not, but through sheer mean-spiritedness!

Well I just don't really like everybody hearing what I've written down. They pinch my ideas. (Y3, f)

Other pupils talked about problems with particular individuals – the prosaic Victor, for instance: 'Victor is one of my friends but he sometimes gets on my nerves. When we're working he puts me off my colouring by saying, "You can't get green walls"' (Y3, f). And boys sometimes have problems with girls: 'Some of the girls are my friends but you don't really work with them because they're always telling you off because they're girls' (Y6, m). Although the reasoning sometimes embodies principles that we may be uneasy about, nevertheless these young people can all offer reasoned explanations for their preferences for particular seating/working patterns.

So far in this section we have given examples, familiar enough, of the way that friends *can* endanger each others' learning. But both our own and earlier research highlight the positive aspects of friendship. Ladd (1990) showed that primary school students with more classroom friends on entering school, students who maintained their friendships over time, and students who readily made new friends, tended to have more favourable perceptions of school as well as higher levels of performance. Epstein (1983) noted that the adolescent peer group is not necessarily a force antagonistic to the school's goals of achievement and academic success, but that 'students both low and high in achievement are positively and cumulatively influenced on achievement by high-achieving friends' (p. 198). And Wentzel and Caldwell (1997) confirm the common-sense argument that positive, work-oriented groups and pairs strengthen achievement because members offer each other assistance. Hartup (1996) said that 'friends provide one another with cognitive and social scaffolding' – or, as a Year 3 pupil put it, 'Friends are not there just to muck about with but to help.'

Indeed, sometimes pupils expressed genuine disappointment that some of their friends were not good working partners – whether because they were talkative or just not very good at responding to the demands of a particular task. At the same time they were clear about the sort of qualities a friend should have to be a good working partner: being prepared to listen was seen as important, caring about school work, being able to explain things, being funny and tolerant – and being ready to help when you are having difficulties. 'Working at the same standard' was also considered important by some friends whereas others accepted an asymmetry in their relationships and were used to one partner offering and the other receiving help; however, they recognized that this pattern of reciprocity might change with different tasks.

Older students talked about needing a friend they could turn to in subjects – not just social situations – that they found difficult, particularly if they were in a top set:

> I think it is important to sit with them in Maths because I am in set one and it's quite hard for me, I'm not naturally talented at Math, I have to work very hard to stay in set one, and I need my friends to help me. (Y10, f)

In a similar situation – but one where he has no close friend, this boy decides what the best strategy is for him:

> I've got this little thing in my head saying that I don't want any help because I don't want to seem small and dumb to them, so the best way is to just keep quiet. (Y10, m)

Students can be uneasy in the often smaller classes of Years 10 and 11 – especially when they are discussion-based – of exposing their failure to understand and to judge what counts as a relevant contribution. This can be a particular problem when pupils are in high sets but find the learning a struggle. Instructional teaching does not publicly expose differences of understanding within the student group – except in question and right-answer sessions; the assignment is where individual strengths and weaknesses show themselves, and the assignment is subject, usually, only to a private viewing by the teacher. So, if you are in 'a high-caste, high-powered set', you are likely to 'just shut up, stay in the background, and if you don't understand it, keep your mouth shut!' (Rudduck and Hopkins, 1984, p. 28). For more advanced work to be effective and allow students to try out ideas, a climate must be established in which talk is seen as an appropriate medium for exploring what people don't understand and not merely for parading what they do understand.

Younger students are also aware of – and speak warmly about – the help they receive at school from their friends:

> Working with a friend gives you ideas and comfort. (Y3, m)

> You do better work with your friends 'cos you can help each other and it will be better – more details and stuff. (Y3, m)

> In my maths I can ask my friends and help my friends. And in my literacy, because I have got a quick mind, I can normally tell the others what to do and how to do it. (Y3, f)

> I prefer working in a pair, with my friend, because me and him share a lot of things in common so we know a lot about different sorts of things, so I can work with him and feel confident about what I'm doing. (Y6, m)

> She comes up with good ideas and we work well together. We generally do chat but we do get our work done together. (Y6, m)

For these primary school children, therefore, *friends who work well together* are a valued part of their picture of school. Older children also value the help they receive from their friends at school, including support with classwork and homework:

> I think I mainly work better at secondary school at the moment than I have in my first school because we are helping each other more often. (Y8, m)

> In maths we talk to each other and we try and see how you do it and then we give each other ideas on how to do stuff ... we don't really do homework together, but we phone each other up and say how do you do this and stuff like that. (Y8, f)

*

One of the idiosyncracies of our education system is that our aspiration for young people to learn to get on with each other and work together productively is to some extent countered by the strong age segmentation of schooling – so that Year 8s and Year 9s see new Year 7s as victims rather than as allies. And again, attempts to foster mutual understanding and collaboration through group work are challenged by an examination system which privileges individual rather than cooperative effort; the outcomes are usually deliberately dis-aggregated so that 'individual effort' can be assessed – the parts rather than the whole. The devaluing of group effort contradicts some of the principles that underlie the concept of the school as a learning community. Putnam and Borko (2000, p. 5) argue that pro-social skills and familiarity with a shared way of working are a good foundation for learning beyond school; but so long as schools remain pre-occupied with individual achievement, then the process of learning in school may not transfer easily to learning beyond school.

What we have tried to do in this section is to demonstrate, through extensive quotation, the interesting variations in the way that young people see the social and academic aspects of schooling and, in particular, how they think about friendships and learning. The data also indicate the extent to which pupils know their own vulnerabilities and whether or not they feel that they can manage them without the teacher's intervention, as well as the analytic way in which some pupils can match the qualities that individual friends possess with the requirements of particular tasks.

4   A Broad Advocacy: Individuals And Movements

Why, in the present climate, is pupil perspective and participation gaining ground in schools, as it undoubtedly is? In this chapter we first discuss the arguments in support of pupil voice coming from a range of people in this country and abroad and then look at three key national initiatives or movements that have helped to give pupil voice a high profile: the children's rights movement, the school improvement movement and citizenship education.

Support from a range of advocates

Support for pupil voice comes from a range of people – educationists, researchers in different social science disciplines, policy makers, teachers, headteachers and of course from pupils themselves.

There are some minority arguments in support of pupil participation and voice. For instance, Holdsworth (2001, p. 2), an Australian academic involved in youth and community work, stresses the proven value of participation *in other social and professional arenas*:

> There's a huge body of evidence: work in the areas of resiliency, health and well-being, etc. ... that emphasises the critical nature of participation to individual and societal health: organisational studies that emphasise the need for participation as a pre-cursor of effective decision-making; studies that highlight participation as a right underlying the development of peaceful, tolerant and productive communities.

Then there is the *bandwagon appeal* – a realization that 'everyone else is into this and so we'd better get our act together'. It became increasingly clear that England lagged behind other countries in terms of ratifying and implementing the articles of the 1989 Convention on the Rights of the Child. This initial tardiness has now given way to a range of initiatives that are supportive of pupil voice but, of course, policies prompted by concerns about 'keeping up' with our neighbours, without an authentic endorsement of key values, tend to rely on coercion rather than commitment in their implementation – and they can be superficial.

The main advocacies cluster around this set of closely related issues:

- the importance of helping students to develop their identities and individual voices;
- the need for young people to be able to 'speak out' about matters that concern them;
- a recognition that in the task of change, pupils are the 'expert witnesses';
- the need for policy makers and schools to understand and respect the world of young people.

There is a fifth, the importance of preparing young people to be citizens in a democratic society, but this is discussed in *Movements that support pupil perspective and participation*, below.

Advocacy that focuses on young people's developing identity

The importance of 'developing identity' for students is vividly explained by Jessye, a student taking part in the collaborative project co-ordinated by Shultz and Cook-Sather which was about helping young people 'to express in their own voices their perceptions, feelings and insights about school' (2001, p. xi). Jessye co-authored a report called *Speaking out loud: girls seeking self-hood* and in it she explains how important it is to find out who you are:

> This [report] is not an explanation of who we are, but rather, a sharing of our battle to find that person, and this is about school because 'student' is part of who we are, 'learning' is part of what we do, and school is where who we are and want to be collides with who everyone else is. [It's] where we attempt to learn who we are and begin to understand who we want to be. (Jessye, p. 39)

Erickson and Schultz (1992, p. 481) argue that 'developing voice' is an important way of helping young people form 'a critical awareness of their own needs and capacities in learning'; they suggest that more interactive pedagogies in the classroom would give pupils a greater chance to find and learn to use their voice. The pupils we have talked with are in agreement. Many are concerned about understanding the nature of their agency and they want to find their own position on issues rather than feel that their views are constructed out of exam-acceptable voices – as a young American woman explains:

> I have seen too many people trapped by listening to the voices in their heads that are not their own, reaching the miserable point when their own voices are lost for good amongst all the jumble. (Julia; in Shultz and Cook-Sather, 2001, p. xi).

Other students talk powerfully about similar experiences, feeling that their voice is ignored or even suppressed in school and about how difficult it is to learn to think for themselves. MacBeath and Weir (1991) home in on 'the powerful influence of external examinations in motivating pupils to "reproduce" learning rather than develop their own thinking'; the following comment is from a UK student:

> When I was younger I was quite ambivalent about God. I didn't care about religion either way. Now religion is put on us in such a forceful way that we violently disbelieve out of spite … We should not be told what to believe. Our opinion is never asked for and never matters. (Y11, f; Mary Earl's field work data, 2001)

Pupils also talk about the lack of occasions when they can discuss teaching and learning; here, another American student explains the feeling of frustration:

> Sometimes I wish I could sit down with one of my teachers and just tell them what I exactly think about their class. It might be good, it might be bad, it's just that you don't have the opportunity to do it. (Anub; in Shultz and Cook-Sather, 2001, p. xii)

Shultz and Cook-Sather (2001, pp. 3–4) summarize the insights arising from their work with 29 middle and high school students. First, students want to have 'more human and humane interactions in school' – and this means greater 'care, respect and support from their teachers, peers and others who influence their educational experience'. Second, students want to be 'their whole selves' – not 'fragmented, categorized, compared to and judged against one another'.

Alongside the aspiration to develop as an individual is the concern to understand the frameworks in school which shape people's expectations of you. Cullingford (1991) interviewed more than 100 English students and concluded that they rarely had opportunities to talk about why they were going to school, or why schooling was the way it was; such issues, he says, were simply not opened up with young people. And Levin, researcher and policy maker from Canada, goes further, commenting that when we hear what students identify as the main elements of schooling – 'memorisation and passing tests' – we realize 'that we have failed to communicate our broader goals and aspirations for schooling in ways that enable young people to understand what learning is for and how it is "for them"' (1999).

Advocacy that focuses on the need for young people to be able to speak out

The issue of students being able to give voice to their concerns is prominent in Apple and Beane's book, *Democratic Schools* (1999, p. 15); they argue that educators should help young people to 'seek out a range of ideas and to voice their own'. Given the crowdedness of the curriculum and the current preoccupation with performance targets teachers might well think that this is only possible if a special space is identified – and such a space might be found in citizenship education where it is acceptable for students to debate issues whose relevance extends beyond the boundaries of the school.

More controversial, however, is how students can communicate their views about practices *within* the school that they feel uneasy about, especially those that seem to them to contradict basic principles of fairness and respect for persons. Young people feel that they have a lot to contribute to the improvement of teaching and learning but to the extent that their stories locate the problems in teachers rather than in themselves they are uncertain how to proceed and tend to remain silent – unless a visiting researcher provides a one-off outlet for talk or writing, as happened in the following two cases. First, a comment from an English pupil, white, female and aged 13:

One of my teachers, she is completely biased to girls. She doesn't like boys and it's not really very good because the boys never get asked for questions, they never get picked for to do examples … And, I mean, obviously she does comment on them if they do something really well, because you can't really ignore something, but … if they say a joke … instead of saying 'Oh well done, that was quite funny' cos the whole class laughs she tells them off for making it funny when it's meant to be a comical bit of work. So she's just a bit biased towards them. (Caroline Lanskey, fieldwork data, 2001)

An African-American male student recalls a similar problem:

[There's one teacher who] would try to embarrass and give a hard time to the white students while she would go easy on the black students. [For example] she would give the third degree to a white student who made excuses about homework and not question the black student. I know students who get her in class and try to change classes because they do not feel like going through that discrimination. They would rather get a teacher who is much harder academically than sit in this teacher's class. (Shultz and Cook-Sather, 2001, p. 66)

Shultz and Cook-Sather argue passionately that 'it is crucial to listen to what students have to say because until we truly understand what students are experiencing – what and how education means, looks, and feels to them – our efforts at school reform will not go very far' (2001, p. 2). But the relative absence, until recently, of structures that legitimate voice, together with the existence of traditional power structures in classroom and school, makes talking and 'telling' difficult.

Students sometimes say that there is no way that they could discuss their criticisms directly with the teachers whose approach troubles them and they are reluctant to inform other teachers, sometimes because they fear reprisal if the teacher concerned finds out about their criticism, or simply because their code of conduct does not allow 'telling on others' or 'sneaking': 'I could talk about what I didn't like about education [but] I can't just go off here and tell everybody … I can't go around telling them anything like that' (Amy, in Shultz and Cook-Sather, 2001, p. 94). It takes time and patient commitment to build open and dependable structures within schools which will enable students and teachers, as partners, and without embarrassment, to talk about what gets in the way of progress in particular classes.

Advocacy that focuses on students' right, as 'expert witnesses', to be consulted about learning

A number of advocates point to the absence in schools of structures for planning improvement that take account of pupils' views as 'expert witnesses' whose testimony needs to be heard. Edwards and Hattam (2000, p. 6) argue that 'Students are the experts on their own lives in and out of schools'; they go on: 'Students can and should participate, not only in the construction of their own learning environments, but as research partners in examining questions of learning and anything else that happens in and around schools.' They quote Delpit (1988, p. 297) who maintained that students themselves are the 'only authentic chroniclers of their own experience'. And Hall and Martello (1996, p. 72) argue, in similar vein, that adults can't and 'don't know better than kids' how kids think and feel about school: 'Too often the assumption is made that children are unable to articulate the complex meta-cognitive that goes on inside their own minds'; a consequence is that adults taking this position believe that there is no point in consulting pupils directly.

Levin observes that much school reform 'is planned and implemented by adults' and that by talking with students 'we can learn more about how classroom and school processes can be made more powerful' – and more engaging. He goes on:

- students have unique knowledge and perspectives that can make reform efforts more successful and improve their implementation;
- students' views can help mobilize staff and parent opinion in favour of meaningful reform;
- constructivist learning, which is increasingly important to high standards reforms, requires a more active student role in schooling;
- students are the producers of school outcomes, so their involvement is fundamental to all improvement (Levin, 1999).

And Holdsworth's advocacy is very similar in tone and emphasis; he argues that we have traditionally relegated young people 'to a less significant realm than those who have reached "adult" life' and that by doing so we obscure both the richness of their experience and their capacity to do more than schools routinely expect and allow (2001, p. 2).

Advocacy that focuses on the need for schools to understand and respect the world of young people

Many students want learning to be more connected to their lives outside school. A nice example, relating to the marking of examination scripts, appeared in the *Guardian* (National News, p. 6, 17 August 2002). In the exam pupils were asked to write a letter to a friend and one did so using text message language. A senior examiner commented that 'the script raised difficult questions' and a spokeswoman for the DfES was reported as saying – with an odd *non sequitur*, 'Text message language holds no sway with us. There is no place for slang in exam papers.' But this, after all, is how many students nowadays communicate with each other. A more appropriate response would have been to require the examiners to 'get real' but it seems that pupils should have known that examiners were looking for more traditional sentence structures!

Gilbert and Robins (1998) offer a persuasive advocacy for student voice on the grounds that policy makers at national and at school level need to be in touch with the reality of young people's lives today:

> This combination of the numbing and ineffective standardization in the schools and the seemingly overwhelming societal forces placed upon students cries for an immediate remedy. That remedy is the inclusion of the student perspective. Since students are the subject of policy, the greater the understanding of student realities, the better and more effective will be the policy created. Teachers and administrators must answer to many constituencies in addition to complex bureaucracies. The realities of students should not be overlooked in the process. (Gilbert and Robins, 1998, p. 3)

And Hodgkin, who is a strong advocate for the participation of young people in educational decision-making and planning, argues that pupils themselves have a huge potential contribution to make, not as passive objects but as active players in the education system. Any legislation concerning school standards will be seriously weakened if it fails to recognise the importance of that contribution. (Hodgkin, 1998, p. 11)

Our own evidence, from diverse school settings, suggests that pupils who are involved in school and who feel that they are respected as individuals and as an institutional and social group are likely to feel a greater sense of respect and belonging, and are less likely to disengage from the school's purposes. A deputy head from one of our projects sums it up: 'You involve the students more in school; do they therefore become more positive towards school? Yes, they do. Do they perform better? Most probably they do; I don't think you need a research project to say that.'

Movements that support pupil perspectives and participation

In this section we move from the range of arguments that have been put forward as a justification for strengthening pupils' participation in schools and look at the ways in which pupil voice is embedded in three movements or initiatives that currently have a high profile. Some of these have, in fact, a long and somewhat chequered history but they have re-surfaced with a new vigour.

The Children's Rights Movement

In order to understand current attitudes to pupil participation and pupil voice we have to look briefly at the progress of the children's rights movement in earlier years. Children's rights have mainly, but not exclusively, been argued for by adults on behalf of pupils and have been pursued in social and welfare arenas as well as in education. The children's rights movement has 'a rich and substantial heritage' (Franklin and Franklin, 1996, p. 96); activity has been high profile at different times and for different reasons but because, Proteus-like, the movement has changed its concerns and its constituencies, its impact has not really been cumulative. The movement has been most at risk from those who hold traditional views of the place of the child in school and in society.

The first formal Declaration of the Rights of the Child in 1924 focused on support for children who lost families and homes in the 1914–18 war; the next Declaration came 35 years later (see Boyden, 1997). The main concerns of such initiatives were conditions *outside* school but there have been some attempts to focus directly on young people's experiences *in school*. In the early 1970s there were two initiatives worth mentioning in this brief sketch – one taken by young people themselves. In autumn 1972 the outcome of a national conference for the National Union of School Students (NUSS, a group formed, for a short time only, within the NUS) was a policy statement which, according to Wagg (1996, p. 14), 'must rank as one of the most uncompromising and idealistic statements of liberation philosophy ever seen in British educational politics'. It is interesting that pupils themselves focus more on aspects of school organization than they do on the curriculum, teaching and learning.

The NUSS document called, among other things, for:

- The speedy abolition of corporal punishment and the prefect system, and … an increase of student responsibility and self discipline in schools.
- All forms of discipline to be under the control of a school committee and all school rules to be published.
- … the abolition of compulsory uniform … , students having the right to determine their own appearance at school.
- … free movement in and out of the school grounds and buildings during break, lunchtime and free periods.
- … school students of all ages to have a 'Common Room' and to have facilities of relaxation similar to those enjoyed by teachers and sixth-formers. (Wagg, 1996, pp. 14–15; there were 27 items in all)

Ironically, some of these items are still on pupils' agenda 30 years later.

In 1975, Lawrence Stenhouse, director of the Humanities Curriculum Project (which defined new and controversial roles for teachers and pupils) drew up a statement of the 'demands' that pupils should be able to make of the school and the expectations that they could justifiably hold of it. The work was commissioned by the then Schools Council but the Council refused, largely because of the radical tone, to give the principles its imprimatur; they were instead published later by the author. These are some of the items that Stenhouse thought would make a difference to young people's experience of school; they are similar in focus and spirit to those in the NUSS document:

Pupils have a right to demand:
- that the school shall treat them impartially and with respect as persons;
- that the school's aims and purposes shall be communicated to them openly, and discussed with them as the need arises;
- that the procedures and organizational arrangements of the school should be capable of rational justification and that the grounds of them should be available to them.

Pupils have a right to expect:
- that the school will offer them impartial counsel on academic matters, and if they desire it, with respect to personal problems;
- that the school will make unabated efforts to provide them with the basic skills necessary for living an autonomous life in our society;
- that the school will do its best to make available to them the major public traditions in knowledge, arts, crafts and sports, which form the basis of a rich life in an advanced society;
- that the school will enable them to achieve some understanding of our society as it stands and that it will equip them to criticise social policy and contribute to the improvement of society. (Stenhouse, 1975a; 1983, pp. 153–4)

The activities of the early 1970s, characterized by Franklin and Franklin (1996, p. 96) as the struggle for 'libertarian participation rights', took schools as the arena for action and the discourse was essentially about empowering students. However, the International Year of the Child, in 1979, moved the children's rights movement away from formal education, re-centred it in child protection and re-located it in the social and welfare arena. Ten years later, the United Nations Convention on the Rights of the Child brought the issues of protection and participation together: it linked the right of young people to talk about their experiences and be heard, and their right to express a view about actions that might be taken in relation to them. According to Freeman (1996, p. 36) this was 'the first convention to state that children have a right to "have a say" in processes affecting their lives'. It proposed that 'the child who is capable of forming his or her own views' should be able to 'express those views freely' in all matters affecting him or her, 'the views of the child being given due weight in accordance with their age and maturity (*ibid*.). Freeman comments:

> The right enunciated here is significant not only for what it says, but because it recognises the child as a full human being with integrity and personality and the ability to participate freely in society ... The views of children are to count [in relation to] decisions ranging from education to environment, from social security to secure accommodation, from transport to television. (1996, p. 37)

The rights movement has enabled us to confront the implications of a situation that we have for too long seen as 'the natural order of things':

> The UN Convention ... has offered a rallying point ... it also offers a programme of proposals designed to empower children and young people. The future of children's rights ... is uncertain in the current political climate with its emphasis on retreating from any progressive policy. But the hope must surely be that in ... the next phase, children will be the key political actors, seeking to establish their rights to protection but also their rights to participate in a range of settings which extend beyond the social and welfare arenas ... The future is open. (Hodgkin, 1998, p. 111)

One of the problems of initiatives that highlight the concept of 'rights' is that they tend to elicit traditionalist responses – flurries of letters in national newspapers arguing that young people should learn to 'be responsible' before they are 'given' rights. The Children's Rights Movement highlighted issues of consultation and participation but it was within the school improvement movement and, later, within the Citizenship Education initiative, that pupil voice found a safe haven.

The school improvement movement

> Students have unique knowledge and perspectives that can make reform efforts more successful and improve their implementation. (Levin, 1999)

The idea of consulting pupils gained support within the school improvement movement largely, perhaps, because it was seen to fit within the standards agenda. We saw, earlier, some of the issues that pupil consultation has helped to put on the school – and indeed, the national – agenda. While the school improvement movement endorses pupil perspectives to the extent that listening to pupils provides a path to the raising of standards, concern with the empowerment of young people was not always seen as part of the acceptable package – although citizenship education provides an umbrella under which empowerment issues might justifiably be tackled. The improvement movement was important for pupil voice because it conferred a legitimacy that enabled teachers to take the first steps towards finding out what pupils had to say about teaching and learning: it offered a practical agenda for change. Sonia Nieto, from the USA, brought pupil voice right into the centre of the school improvement frame when she said this:

> Reforming school structures alone will not lead to differences in student achievement ... if such changes are not accompanied by profound changes in how we as educators think about our students. One way to begin the process of changing school policies is to listen to students' views about them. (Nieto, 1994, pp. 395 and 396)

To manage school improvement we need to look at schools from the pupils' perspective and that means tuning in to their experiences and views and creating a new role for them as active participants in their own learning and within the school as a learning community. For instance (as we saw in Chapter 2), they have things to say about the appointment of new teachers:

> If they are thinking about what kind of teachers to hire, they should
> ask the students ... There are so many things in the school that they're
> trying to fix but they're trying to fix it the way *they* want it. (Fredo,
> in Shultz and Cook-Sather, 2001, p. 84)

However, in focusing on pupil voice we should remember that
teachers may feel that *their* voice also needs to be taken more account
of – particularly by policy makers and particularly in relation to the
flow of school improvement initiatives that are designed at the centre
and then sent out to 'the provinces' for teachers to implement.

Another source of legitimation, at least within the research community, were the questions being asked about pupils by educationists
from other countries. In the 1970s, Paul Willis had commented on
the so-called 'crisis in education': the debate, which focused on
definitions of standards and the impact on learning of progressive
methods, is remarkable, he said, 'for the absence of the views of both
classroom teachers and pupils'. Twenty years later, similar comments
were being made by eminent educationists from other education
systems and this provided some lateral support for policy makers
and teachers who were cautious about venturing down the path of
pupil participation. For example, in Canada, Michael Fullan asked,
in relation to school reform: 'What would happen if we treated the
student as someone whose opinion mattered ... ?' (1991, p. 170). In
the United States, Erickson and Schultz pointed out that 'virtually no
research has been done that places student experience at the centre
of attention' (1992, p. 476), and Nieto, also from the USA, observed
that 'research that focuses on student voice is relatively recent and
scarce' (1994, p. 396). In Sweden, Andersson said that 'politicians
who decide about school reforms and the teachers who run the
classrooms seldom ask how the students themselves perceive their
school' (1995, p. 5) and Levin, from Canada, noted that while the
literature on school-based management 'advocates more important
roles for teachers and parents ... students are usually omitted from
the discussion' (1995, p. 17).

Nieto also pointed out that pupils' views have, for the most part,
been missing 'in discussions concerning strategies for confronting
educational problems' and, importantly, that 'the voices of students
are rarely heard in the debates about school failure and success'

(1994, p. 396). This view was echoed by Suzanne Soo Hoo (1993, p. 392) who said that 'Traditionally, students have been overlooked as valuable resources in the restructuring of schools'. Patricia Phelan and her colleagues (also from North America) argued that it is important to give attention to students' views of things that affect their learning – not so much factors outside school but those in school that teachers and policy makers have some power to change (1991, p. 696).

Support for looking at the world of the school from the pupil perspective and for enhancing pupil participation intensified in the 1990s with the advent of the school improvement movement but it was there well before that in the writings of individual educationists. For example, in the USA, Silberman was writing in 1971 in a way that pre-figured the argument for involving pupils more closely in school improvement efforts:

> If schooling is to make sense to children, let alone appeal to them, we must assume responsibilities. First, we should carefully examine the experiences that students undergo. The examination of experiences which result from institutional aspects of school life is especially urgent because they have received superficial study up 'til now. Second, we must make a conscious decision to alter conditions that create undesirable experiences. Third, we must communicate clearly to students the goals and expectations we believe make sense. And, fourth, we should affirm the right of students to negotiate our purposes and demands so that the activities we undertake with them have greatest possible meaning to all. (Silberman, 1971, p. 364)

In the UK, at about the same time as Silberman was writing, David Hargreaves (1967) and Colin Lacey (1970) published their influential case studies of schools and 'gave a powerful impetus to interest in children's views of their everyday life' (Prout and James, 1997, p. 19). Peter Woods' research (1980; 1981) strengthened the legitimacy and usefulness of focusing on pupils' perspectives and there were numerous other individual studies that gathered data directly from pupils. Although not having the force of a movement, these separate initiatives laid the foundations for later work.

Interestingly, John Gray (1990) gave the pupil perspective a central place in the early debate about performance: at a time when performance indicators were breeding like rabbits he made a case for only three – and two of the three not only focused on pupils' experiences of schooling but required schools to consult pupils in order to arrive at an analysis of the situation. During the last decade research focusing on pupil perspective and participation has grown at a remarkable pace and policy makers have also become increasingly alert to the wisdom – or prudence – of taking account of pupils' experiences of learning (the QCA has commissioned work on pupil perspectives on assessment, on different curriculum subjects and on the national curriculum, and the DfES has emphasized the importance of the pupil perspective in many of the research projects that it is now funding).

While it is now increasingly acceptable to listen to what pupils have to say about schooling, we need to remember what Gill Jones wrote in her summary of the Joseph Rowntree work on youth in transition (2002): 'Policy makers must recognise that giving young people a voice does not necessarily empower them; what it can do, and is doing, however, is providing a more realistic agenda for improving the conditions of learning.'

Citizenship education

The resurgence of interest in citizenship education has also supported the idea of greater pupil participation in school; it is also the only nationally endorsed curriculum initiative that is about pupil empowerment, albeit somewhat indirectly, rather than just school improvement.

The 1998 Report of the Government's Advisory Group, *Education for Citizenship and the Teaching of Democracy in Schools* (known as the Crick Report), argued the need for citizenship education to be part of the formal curriculum:

> We unanimously advise the Secretary of State that citizenship and the teaching of democracy ... is so important both for schools and the life of the nation that there must be a statutory requirement for schools to ensure that it is part of the entitlement of all pupils. (Crick, 1998, p. 7)

The words of the Lord Chancellor are invoked (p. 8) to give more weight to the argument (although his credibility in speaking for the citizenry is somewhat questionable): 'Unless we become a nation of engaged citizens, he said, 'our democracy is not secure.'

But the task of 'teaching democracy' in schools is a considerable challenge. Past experience is not entirely encouraging: citizenship education in one form or another has existed for well over a hundred years but its development has not been steady and cumulative. It has undergone numerous changes of identity and name – civic duty, civics education, modern studies, social studies, political literacy, political competence, and now, citizenship education. What is good about the present term is that it opens the way for a focusing not just on the institution of government but also the institution of the school; it signals an interest not only in the framework of laws and arrangements within which individuals and groups act, but also in the people themselves and the significance of the ways in which they interact.

Schools have not in the main developed as democratic institutions. Indeed the spirit of community and democratic practice has tended to flourish more in school settings that are relatively free from state control. As part of our project, *Consulting Pupils about Teaching and Learning*, Caroline Lanskey looked at readily accessible accounts of three well-known 'progressive' independent schools: Bedales and King Alfred School (founded in the 1890s) and the White Lion School (see Lanskey *et al.*, 2002; the summaries below are based on her research).

What these schools appear to have had in common is a strong commitment to the idea of the self-governing body and to student voice, autonomy and responsibility. Critical reviews of the impact of the principles that unite these schools are difficult to come by; accounts are often written by founding members or headteachers who tend to take an advocacy line. However, in the present climate of concern about citizenship education it is worth revisiting such schools to see how their values were expressed within the daily life of the school and contributed to a sense of community and democratic practice.

Bedales, founded in 1893 (and co-educational from 1898) was one of a group of pioneering boarding schools known as 'new schools'. The founding philosophy emphasized 'freedom, trust, responsibility' as 'the cornerstone of education'. Students had a role in the organization of the school, participated fully in the monitoring of personal progress, and had some choice in learning activities. Badlay, the founder, wanted a 'true community' rather than 'a herd' and felt it important that 'the members feel that they have a share in its government and the organisation of its life'. The school parliament was an advisory rather than a legislative body and, importantly, it was set up so that 'Staff and the School may understand each others' point of view and learn the reasons why any particular measure is necessary or where it would press hardly'. The founder believed that 'if we want them [students] to be trustworthy we must show them that they are trusted'. There was a strong commitment to the encouragement of responsibility for one's own learning and on two afternoons a week students could choose their own activity. Interestingly, in the library, which was a central feature of school life, each student was allocated his or her own seat and given many opportunities for working there.

King Alfred School was founded in 1898 by members of the Fabian Society in north London. Student participation was strongly evident through a system of self-government including the management of one's own learning. The Dalton plan, which was developed in the USA in 1916 and reached England a few years later, reinforced the school's founding principles. The Dalton plan emphasized the value of co-operative working and the development of students' social skills within a framework of communal responsibility for learning and living. Specialist subject rooms were known as laboratories where students could 'experiment'. There was no fixed timetable and students were encouraged to draw up their own schedule by examining strong and weak subjects and allocating time to each as they thought fit. These principles became embedded in the practices of the King Alfred School as a later head teacher commented: 'We believe in the educational value of personal liberty' and our aim is 'to develop an independent attitude and to encourage in children a sense of responsibility for their own work and behaviour'. Students had a contract with the teacher to study the subjects in the order they preferred provided that they covered an agreed amount of work on every subject by the end of each term. Allowing children to work at their own pace was an important feature of the organization of learning.

The White Lion School opened in 1972; 10 years later, under the auspices of the London Education Authority, it became the only

State-funded Free School, but closed in 1990 because, now under the Islington Borough Council, it felt unable, or disinclined, to deliver the National Curriculum. Similar values informed practices at the White Lion School as at the two school profiled above:

> The *White Lion Free School* took up to 50 children from nursery to school leaving age and was run as a collective with the teachers known as 'workers' and the children as 'kids'. Autonomy was central to the school's approach to learning: 'for us learning is ... the development of the capacity for choice and control ... it requires a certain essential degree of freedom within which the learner's own needs can be met ... the freedom to make significant choices between positive activities ... we think that to force a child to do something is to remove the very autonomy which is essential for learning'. Students were expected to participate actively in the management of their learning and had a say in the day-to-day running of the school, a choice of what and when to learn and a say in the evaluation of their learning.

Today, again, the principles and practices of pupil voice – which are about both consultation and participation – are very close to the principles and practices envisaged for citizenship education. Both initiatives appear to be interested in:

- supporting active rather than passive involvement;
- supporting informed thought and action rather than simply reactive compliance;
- supporting the analytic understanding of the structures and rules of institutions which young people are members of;
- supporting a reasoned balance between rights and responsibilities;
- taking into account the views of others on social issues;
- enabling younger and older pupils to be able to make a contribution to the well being of their community and providing opportunities for them to do so;
- respecting the right of the individual to express a seriously held view on matters that affect him or her.

Pupil consultation can help to meet at least four of the key dimensions of citizenship education:

- skills of participation;
- responsible action;
- skills of enquiry; and
- skills of communication.

It can also support the fifth, the acquisition of knowledge – although somewhat indirectly – in that pupils who are involved feel trusted, and have some sense of control over what is happening are more likely to commit themselves to learning.

In schools today the most manageable contexts for consultation are probably these:

- an occasional 'referendum' where the opinions of pupils in one or all year cohorts are canvassed by teachers via questionnaires or discussion forums or via their representatives on the school or pupil council;
- a regular forum (such as Circle Time, the Year Council, or Headteacher's Question Time) where pupils in a class or in a year group can talk about what is on their mind;
- an occasional series of small group discussions about how members of a particular sub-group of pupils (the disengaged, the high achievers, the girls, the boys, for example) can talk about the conditions of learning in school and what might be done to support their progress;
- an enquiry designed by teachers and pupils which involves pupils in gathering the view of their peers (via, say, a short structured interview or questionnaire), analysing the data and summarizing the outcomes for their peers and for their teachers.

What matters, whatever the arena, is that there is some feedback to pupils who are involved or represented so that they know what will happen as a result of their observations.

The topics listed below are ones that pupils have been consulted about and that are potentially relevant to the agenda of citizenship education. They are essentially about helping young people to understand and help shape and/or sustain the learning community that they are members of; several of them highlight questions about pupils' accountability to each other and about the social conditions of life in a community.

Pupils have been consulted about school-wide issues, such as:

- revising the school mission statement;
- changing the system of rewards;
- revising the content and presentation of the school rules;
- strategies for minimizing bullying in the playground;
- qualities needed in a new caretaker or meals supervisor;
- school uniform;
- ways of giving each year an identity;
- getting the school council to work well.

Pupils have been consulted about year group issues, such as:

- planning an end-of-Year 9 induction to the work of Year 10;
- improving the status of Year 8;
- the contents of an induction booklet for new pupils;
- how best to organize parents' evenings;
- qualities needed in a year-tutor;
- what pupils think about targets;
- what pupils think about grouping practices;
- year-group responsibilities for special duties;
- best ways of organizing homework or study support.

Pupils have been consulted about issues in their form or class, such as:

- teacher and peer group behaviours that get in the way of learning;
- how to deal with noise in the classroom;
- seating arrangements;
- how to improve working in groups;
- peer support in learning;
- ways of catching up if you don't understand or miss work.

In relation to some issues, pupils have been invited to summarize their views for the school governors, for the headteacher, or for the senior management team, or to present the outcomes of the consultation to a staff meeting.

The principles that guide such consultations are central to citizenship education: they are about communicating and sustaining a spirit of respect and trust in interactions between teachers and pupils, and sustaining the credibility of the process of consultation itself in the eyes of pupils and teachers.

Principles for teachers:

- that the desire to hear what young people have to say is genuine;
- that the topic is not trivial;
- that the purpose of the consultation, and what it might lead to, is explained to the pupils involved;
- that young people know what will happen to any information they offer;
- that they monitor any imbalance (in terms of class, gender or ethnicity) in the selection of pupils whose views are heard and given attention;
- that young people are confident that expressing a sincerely held opinion, or describing a negative feeling or an experience, will not disadvantage them;
- that feedback is offered to those who have been consulted;
- that action taken is explained and where necessary justified so that young people understand the diversity of views that exist alongside their own, and the broader concerns that shape decisions.

Principles for pupils:

- that what they say is what they really think or feel is a fair reflection of their experience;
- that individual teachers or pupils should not be mentioned by name;
- that they will try to be constructive in their comments;
- that they will listen to and respect the views of other pupils;
- that they will try to see things from the perspective of others;
- that they are prepared to play their part in any collaborative follow-up action designed to improve things that pupils have been worried about.

Tasks for school leaders:

- reassuring staff, parents and governors that consulting pupils is recognized nationally as a legitimate practice that supports the development of citizenship education;
- building up support among staff (who may be sceptical) by presenting evidence of the positive outcomes of consultation;
- being sensitive to the anxiety experienced by teachers who have not before consulted pupils about teaching and learning;
- ensuring that other school policies and initiatives are in harmony with the values that underpin pupil consultation;
- ensuring that various areas of school life offer opportunities for pupils' voices to be heard and that consultation is not confined to the school council.

Teachers working on citizenship education and pupil voice are likely to encounter some common concerns and dilemmas: for instance, concerns about bias and authenticity and about whether we are more interested in young people as future citizens or present citizens. First, the issue of *bias and/or unobtrusive control*. Onora O'Neill said this in her 2002 Reith lectures: 'I might trust the schoolteacher to teach my child arithmetic but not citizenship' (2002, p. 9); her concern was not explained nor expanded on but may reflect earlier concerns about the danger in political education of the subtle transmission of political bias which Bernard Crick examined and discussed (see Crick, 1990, p. 80). The nearest parallel in pupil voice is the concern about adults 'interpreting' what pupils say. It is not easy for adults to understand learning as pupils experience it and even if we try to check out our interpretation with pupils they may be more inclined to agree, because of the power relations, than to question and correct us. Fielding (2002, drawing on Humphries, 1994) goes further: he underlines the often unrecognized – and usually unintended – danger of 'accommodation'; this occurs when challenging ideas offered by pupils are modified by adults so that they conform to and do not disturb the existing orthodoxy. For example, in one school, 17-year-old students wanted to have more say over things that mattered to them but after discussion with senior teachers the agreement limited their influence to being able to choose the colour of the pullovers to be worn by their year group.

A second issue is *the authenticity of policy-level commitment* to both pupil voice and citizenship education. Ahier *et al.* (2003), concentrating on central policy makers, note the 'quite substantial body of commentary [which] has accumulated concerning the *motives* underlying the decision to introduce citizenship education at this point in time, following decades of official neglect or half-hearted commitment' (p. 164). The authors suggest that by highlighting citizenship 'as part of the *content* of education' the government has found 'a convenient way of adding a *social gloss* to an education system which was being reshaped structurally in ways that reinforce individualistic instrumentalism' (pp. 164–5). They also point to the danger, given the current commitment to *active* citizenship, that the alienation and abstentionism of young people might be presented as 'deficits of knowledge and understanding' rather than as problems engendered by institutional inadequacies' (*ibid.*, p. 166). Others have suggested that part of the reason for the government's current interest in citizenship education is evidence of apathy among young voters and the hope that a way can be found of re-igniting their interest in matters of governance.

Holdsworth (2001, pp. 4–5) is also concerned about authenticity of support for pupil participation but more at the school level. He dismisses such easy interpretations of participation as 'bums on seats' and 'taking part in activities organized by adults' in favour of a more demanding student-centred vision. His categories are expressed in terms of 'degrees' of citizenship. He goes on to suggest that 'in working to enable, support or encourage the participation of young people' we are in fact making choices between some radically different perceptions of young people (the four categories below are shortened versions of Holdsworth's originals):

Young people as clients (non-citizen participation):

> we see young people as (un)willing actors in situations we define; participation means 'turning up', 'being there' or 'taking part' in 'our' activities.

Young people as consumers (token participation):

> we see young people as consumers of services; we hear what they are saying in order to target our services better (consultation is market research); we may put a pupil on a committee to help the information gathering.

Young people as minimal citizens (deferred participation):

> young people's citizenship is focused on formal aspects (e.g. learning how to vote, elect, etc.); young people are future or 'apprentice' citizens.

Young people as maximal citizens (full or 'deep' participation):

> young people are recognized as citizens now, with skills and ideas, with valued contributions to make to the school community.

Helping pupils to articulate their views as members of the community of the school is a central feature of citizenship education, along with the related skills and sensitivities of understanding a range of different perspectives on an issue and weighing evidence as a precursor to action.

The third, and perhaps the most important, issue is whether we are focusing on *young people as present or future citizens*; it is about how we prioritize 'now' and 'later'. An argument offered in support of pupil voice is that being able to express an informed view confidently and take account of other views will stand young people in good stead in life beyond school. Similarly, Crick (1990) quotes an advocate of political education who argues that pupils will be 'much better prepared for the change from school to adult and working life' by the new work in school. In neither case is the concern with the here and now of school emphasized, with the perception of school as a micro-society whose system of governance can be explored, understood – and shaped – by its members.

Perhaps the most challenging dimension is *the need for pupils to learn about citizenship in a structure that offers them experience of the principles of citizenship*. The benefits of citizenship education, says the 1998 Report, will be to empower pupils to participate effectively 'in *society*' and 'in *the state*' as active, informed, critical and responsible citizens' (p. 9; emphasis added). While *future* participation in arenas *outside* school are highlighted, there is perhaps insufficient attention to participation in the pupils' *present* community of the school – to the importance of democratic principles being enacted in school, with all that that means for the status of the pupil.

Interestingly, Harold Dent, way back in 1930, argued that pupils will learn not by talking about civics – a futile process – but by living civics in the daily life of the school (see Rudduck, 1999b):

> ... every school is a community already partly organized and wanting only the touch of the expert to turn it into a model of governmental or local administration. Every child might, if the opportunity was seized, live his school life in his miniature State, finding within it a career open to talent, and then pass out into the greater State with a developed and sane comprehension of how the affairs of a community are managed. (Dent, 1930, p. 15)

His view is echoed in the 1990s by Hodgkin: 'Democracy ... is not something which is "taught", it is something which is practised' (1998, p. 11).

Another problem is about building a whole school commitment. Not all schools are ready to 'walk the talk' of citizenship education and pupil voice. What Crick says of citizenship education is true of pupil voice: 'To achieve any sensible objectives, political education has to be seen as a commitment for a school rather than the public-spirited activity of particular teachers.' Both initiatives can create anxiety among teachers through their implicit challenge to the traditional authority of the teacher and the familiar authority structure of the school. As Cook-Sather (2002, p. 3) has recently said, in pupil voice work the challenge of 'authorising students' perspectives' involves changes 'in mindset' as well as 'changes in the structure of educational relationships'; her comment applies also to citizenship education.

As a result of the high profile of citizenship education, more opportunities for pupil consultation and participation will be built into the fabric of the school's structure. But it takes time and very careful preparation to build a climate in which both teachers and pupils feel comfortable working together on the conditions of learning and on the management of learning in schools. Many schools may rely on their school councils and we know that these work well if they are the centre, and symbol, of school-wide democratic practice. If the school is not ready for pupil participation then a school council can become a way of formalizing and channelling students' criticisms – an exercise in damage limitation rather than an opportunity for constructive consultation (see Trafford, 1993). The most recent work of the organization, School Councils UK highlights not just the formal structure of a council but the values that underpin it, and the importance of a climate in which opportunities for consultation and participation are genuinely school-wide and socially inclusive.

We also have to be wary of the 'It's not my area of the curriculum' escape route. Now that citizenship education has found a niche in the national curriculum there may be a temptation for teachers who are already overstretched and who are not involved in 'delivering it' within a specified timetable slot to feel that it is 'being done' and that they are released from further obligation. Similarly, in work on pupil voice, teachers can say that the school council is 'dealing with all that'. By corralling the two initiatives in this way, the tensions or threats that they can present can be minimized but the potential for change will also be limited. In both cases what matters is that the principles and values of pupil voice and participation are threaded through the daily interactions and communications of school life and reflect a coherent and widely supported set of values and principles.

The 1989 Convention on the Rights of the Child helped to legitimate pupil voice both as an element in citizenship education and as a source of guidance in school improvement where it became clear that pupils could provide a practical agenda for change. At government level, key initiatives have been the setting up of the Children and Young People Unit and, more recently, the convening of an advisory group to construct guidance for schools on ways of strengthening the participation of children and young people, both in and out of school.

Whatever the motives that lie behind government support, there is now a national framework and a useful rhetoric that supports both pupil voice and citizenship education.

5   What Kind Of Pupil Do We Want In School?

Historically, the character of 'the pupil' has been largely shaped by the resources of the situation – in particular the economic need to manage quite large numbers of young people with few adults, as in the monitorial system of the nineteenth century. Jones (1990, pp. 57–8) reminds us that such systems were designed to provide cheap instruction for the masses which would help to 'manufacture' a disciplined society. This act of reclamation was dependent, in schools, on a technology of 'observation and examination' (*ibid.*, p. 59).

Ball (1990, p. 159), building on Jones's analysis (and citing Foucault), argues that the product of 'an observing hierarchy' and 'a normalising judgment' is a form of 'surveillance that makes it possible to qualify, to classify, and to punish'. Jones and Ball are talking about a totalizing regime, but even at the level of the classroom the messages were clear: some, for instance, had raked seating which enabled the adult in charge to keep a watchful eye on their many charges. And We have seen, in the old hall of a city grammar school, a sort of one-person watch tower from which all pupils could be viewed by the head and which conveyed the unambiguous message that the adult within was indeed 'monarch of all s/he surveyed' (a version of the 'panopticon technology' that Ball writes about (p. 58) as a symbol of authoritarian command).

In these circumstances the kind of pupil that the school wanted was one who was ready to conform and 'apply' him or herself to the requirements of school work. In the matrix below (see Figure 2), the pupils of this era would be occupying the top left hand quadrant, although 'passive and compliant' might have been a truer description for some than 'passive and positive'.

Figure 2

PASSIVE

Accepting	*Indifferent*
• attends regularly	• mistrusts school and teachers
• quite likes school and teachers	• withdraws from sources of support
• does what is required	• denies concern about progress
• trusts school to deliver a future	• does not look ahead
POSITIVE	**NEGATIVE**
• wants to understand frameworks	• refuses to accept code of conduct
• wants to talk to teachers about problems and progress in learning	• behaviour is anti-social
• is ready to organize things and take more responsibility	• attendance is irregular
• is ready to help other pupils	• frequently on report
	• faces prospect of removal to another class or school
Influencing	*Rejecting*

ACTIVE

Source: adapted from Nixon *et al.* (1996, p. 113)

What kind of pupil do we want today?

The current climate in education was recently characterized by Carol Adams, Chief Executive of the General Teaching Council, as one of heavy workload, initiative overload, target setting and poor pupil behaviour (see Woodward, the *Guardian*, Wednesday, 8 January 2003). In such a climate, teachers might also prefer pupils to be in the top left quadrant – pupils who are 'accepting', who get on quietly and steadily and who, as a body, enable the school to meet its targets. Moreover, teachers themselves might feel that the top left is the space that the government has assigned for *them*, not just for their pupils. However, according to the General Secretary of the Secondary Heads Association, also reported in the Woodward article, many teachers are not necessarily in an 'accepting' mood: '[They] are not prepared to continue to remain quiet in the face of the difficulties that have been imposed on them by successive governments.'

At about the same time as Carol Adams offered her analysis, the editor of the journal *Forum* made an equally strong statement about central directives for change. She said, 'As it happens, teachers are not averse to change that directly benefits all their pupils, and often welcome it, *in contrast to change that is imposed*, for example, just to raise SATs scores or boost league table positions.' And then comes the punchline: 'Annoyingly for the government, it is a distinction [that teachers] find easy to make' (Dixon, 2002, p. 93; emphasis added).

The current requirement for schools to concentrate fairly single-mindedly on raising standards has not, however, totally subdued teachers' commitment to the personal growth of individual students. The schools we have worked closely with over the last four years – and despite differences of tradition and social context – seem to be caught between 'a desire . . . to serve the competitive demands of a stratified society, and a desire . . . to play a socially integrative and democratic role, serving the right of all children to develop to their fullest potential' (Bastian *et al.*, 1985, p. 1). Teachers are learning to manage a degree of cognitive dissonance in order to preserve the right of pupils to position themselves in the lower left hand quadrant – which is where pupil voice would lead them.

Rotter distinguishes between two forms of control, external and internal: people with an *internal locus of control* feel themselves able to determine what happens in their environment while those with an *external locus of control* feel that forces outside themselves are always determining what happens to them. An observation study discussed by Wang (1983) and based on Rotter's framework found that pupils who felt that they were determining events in their lives tended to be 'active and assertive and exhibit a high degree of exploratory behaviour and excitement about learning'; such students are more likely to be in the bottom half of our quadrant, managing either a positive pro-learning stance or sustaining a strenuous anti-learning stance. In contrast, in the study that Wang summarizes, students who felt themselves objectified and merely 'acted on' tended to be relatively 'compliant and non-exploratory' and were often inattentive. These students would take their place in the top left quadrant, a sort of low-energy comfort zone – which is becoming rather full! Pupils here are no trouble: they get on, they do what they are told, and for busy teachers concerned about the increased stress and strain of their professional lives, such qualities in their pupils can, in certain circumstances, seem attractive.

There are other dilemmas in the way we think about students today. One is the tension between the aspiration to have pupils in class *now* who are steady and biddable and the aspiration to help pupils develop the kind of capabilities that will enable them to cope with the complex task of composing a life *beyond school*. As Aronowitz and Giroux said (1986, p. 9), the way forward is not to programme pupils 'in certain directions so that they will behave in set ways' but to help them towards a reasoned and responsible autonomy: the task for schools is to help young people exercise power over their own lives both in school and as an investment for the future.

Out of school, the attributes in the bottom left are widely high-lighted as important – a readiness to take responsibility for organizing things and for helping others, a willingness to ask questions and understand frameworks, a readiness to share with others in positive action. Guy Claxton notes that a pamphlet written as part of the Industrial Society's survey *Speaking Up, Speaking Out*, concluded that 'Schools are seen as failing to equip young people with the ability to learn for life rather than exams' (Claxton, 2001, p. 44). He goes on to argue that the new social and economic conditions demand a flexible way of thinking that many young people in school do not believe they have been helped to develop. And, echoing what we have said earlier in this book, he suggests that the current preoccupations of the curriculum and the tests may weaken young people's 'real life learning power' given that survival and success in 'real life' depends in part on having 'the tools for effective, autonomous learning' (Claxton, 2001, p. 44).

Interestingly, the qualities that Claxton is talking about are compatible with those in the bottom left quadrant – and both come close to those endorsed in the new guidelines for citizenship education (which became a foundation subject in the autumn of 2002). Jerome summarizes the rather vague but virtuous 'official' argument for citizenship education having a place in the national curriculum:

> Citizenship gives pupils the knowledge, skills and understanding to play an effective role in society at local, national and international levels. It helps them to become informed, thoughtful and responsible

citizens who are aware of their duties and rights. It promotes their spiritual, moral, social and cultural development, making them more self-confident and responsible both in and beyond the classroom. It encourages pupils to play a helpful part in the life of their schools, neighbourhoods, communities and the wider world. It also teaches them about our economy and democratic institutions and values; encourages respect for different national, religious and ethnic identities; and develops pupils' ability to reflect on issues and take part in discussions. (2001, p. 8)

What remains somewhat blurred in this statement is, first, the balance between students' contribution to the community of the school and their contribution to society after school, and, second, the balance between students' experiences of democracy now and the experiences of democracy that they will be expected to help sustain beyond school. It is chastening in some ways to go back to Harold Dent who, in 1930, was arguing that 'before you can have an educated democracy you must offer your democracy an education that is likely to make it one' (1930, p. 14); he also offered the simple logic that there is little point in expecting education to deliver the skills and capacities needed for future life if the education itself is one that does not engage pupils.

Osler (1994, p. 146), writing about our schools today, offers a similar message; she claims that running through most of the articles in the United Nations Convention on the Rights of the Child is the principle of participation which involves 'the child acquiring a range of skills, including social skills and skills for communication and judgment'. She goes on, 'The aims of an education compatible with the principles of the Convention must be to empower the child by providing opportunities to practise and develop these skills of participation.' There are strong messages for pedagogy, she says, which may involve 'the individual teacher in a complete reassessment of her or his role'. She also suggests that there are implications for the school as a whole:

Democracy is best learned in a democratic setting where participation is encouraged, where views can be expressed openly and discussed, where there is freedom of expression for pupils and teachers, and where there is fairness and justice. (Osler, 1994, p. 14)

And Lynn Davies reminds us just how tough the democratic agenda is: it entails

> a continuous political process whereby the operations of decision-making are transparent and open to challenge; whereby all members participate in the organization of the school; whereby rules and laws are consensually drawn up and members agree to abide by those contractual rules . . .; and whereby the human rights of all participants are upheld. (1999, p. 39)

There will be, for many schools, a tension between 'teaching *about*' government and democracy and enacting the principles in the democratic community of the school in the way that Davies suggests. For example, about a year ago we talked about the idea of pupil consultation in a democratic framework to a group of senior and headteachers from some very tough inner-city schools. 'Teaching about' was the preferred strategy for citizenship and the idea of developing consultation as part of a school-wide interpretation of the citizenship agenda was parried with these comments:

- Schools *can't* be democratic institutions.
- It *is* important to teach *about* citizenship. Our kids need information – they used to think Maggie Thatcher was the heir to the throne.
- Our kids have such insecurities at home that when they come to school they just want to be told what to do, not given choices or responsibility.
- If you invite pupils to express views at school and they're not allowed to at home then you're in trouble.

For these teachers, trying to do their best in the daily battle between supporting learning and maintaining control, the prospect of more 'freedom' for their pupils to express views and to take action was daunting; neither they nor the students were ready for it.

Indeed, there may be many schools, not all of them working in such exceptionally challenging circumstances perhaps, for whom developing pupil voice within a properly democratic framework is a very big step forward. Wyse (2001) decided to look in two primary and two secondary schools for evidence of such things as children's 'right to express views freely on all matters affecting the child' – which was a key article in the 1989 convention. The study found 'that children's opportunities to express their views were extremely limited even when school councils were in place' and concluded 'that the goal of active citizenship espoused by recent national curriculum developments will remain elusive unless educational practice changes to focus on school processes rather than products' (Wyse, 2001, p. 209). In the schools Wyse studied, there was a fairly familiar impasse between teachers and pupils: pupils didn't feel that teachers wanted to listen to them and said that the influence they had through the school council was limited and trivial; teachers for their part felt that in school, adults should be in control and that only when they get older will children be ready for more rights and responsibilities. Wyse comments:

> If children are to participate fully in their education then their opinions ... are fundamental. There was no evidence [in the case study schools] that children were consulted in any way in relation to their views about the nature of their teaching ... During individual lessons we saw no attempts by teachers to encourage students to evaluate the quality of the activities. (2001, pp. 212–13)

Wyse's sample was small – only four schools in all – and we could match those schools with others that have managed to build up, over time, the beginnings of a new order of experience for young people in school that is founded on principles of democratic participation. But what Wyse's study alerts us to is the extraordinarily difficult task it will be in some settings to enact democratic principles in the daily life of the school, especially in a climate which encourages quick solutions and celebrates rapid turn-arounds. Wyse concluded, significantly, that organizational readiness to hear and to act on pupils' observations about teaching and learning in school fell far short of young people's 'ability to think seriously about complex issues' (*ibid.*, p. 213).

In this chapter we have been exploring what influences our judgments about the kind of pupil we want and there are some key questions. For example, are our images of the pupils we want in school over-influenced by values from the past? Should we instead be working back from the virtues and capacities we want to see in post school-age citizens? Are the virtues we seek in pupils ones that will make for a quiet life in school and classroom but have a limited shelf-life beyond school? Do we have a basic set of values about humankind that we are seeking to distil? Are we looking for study skills or coping skills – and as a preparation for life and lifelong learning or just the exams?

Newman (in Erickson and Schultz, 1992, p. 481) claims that 'the most immediate and persisting issue' in schools is not so much low achievement but students who are disengaged (i.e. students in the bottom right quadrant of our model). Our experience of working with a variety of schools on the project persuades us that opportunities for consultation and for enhanced participation in schools have a direct impact on pupils' engagement. We think it works in this way:

- If pupils feel that they matter in school and that they are respected, then they are more likely to commit themselves to the school's purposes.
- Pupils' accounts of what helps them to learn and what gets in the way of their learning can provide a practical agenda for improving teaching and learning.
- If teaching and the conditions of learning are experienced as congenial then pupils are more likely to commit themselves to learning and develop positive identities as learners.

Figure 3 is a diagrammatic presentation of our argument.

More opportunities for talking about learning can help pupils to understand their own learning and working habits so that they feel more in control of their learning – and this in turn seems to enhance their motivation and engagement. Where pupils are committed to school and engaged in the learning tasks, then they are more likely to invest energy in managing their own learning well – and they will expect more exciting and productive experiences in lessons.

Figure 3

PUPIL CONSULTATION AND PARTICIPATION

yields practical   strengthens
agenda   pupil self-esteem

**ENHANCED COMMITMENT TO
LEARNING AND TO SCHOOL**

sustained by
transformation of teachers' knowledge of pupils
(greater awareness of their capacity for constructive analysis)

transformation of   *transformation of teacher–*
pedagogic and   *pupil relationships (from*
organizational   *passive or oppositional to*
practices   *more active and*
                             collaborative)

What conditions of learning do pupils want in schools?

Although this chapter started with a discussion of different perspectives on the kind of pupil adults want in schools and in society,
it is also important to ask what kind of pupil *pupils* want to be – and
to consider how the conditions of learning in schools influence what
pupils can be.

Interviews with pupils in primary and secondary schools across
the country confirm that pupils are interested in changing the
regimes and relationships that cast them in a marginal role and that
limit their agency. Pupils of all ages ask for more autonomy, they
want school to be fair and they want pupils, as individuals and as
an institutional group, to be regarded as important members of the

school community. Policy makers may think about school primarily in terms of lessons and formal learning but for young people school is a holistic experience: it is about lessons, it is about what happens between lessons, it is about relationships and it is about who and what is valued by the school.

The fragments of testimony that we gathered in interviews appear to be linked by a set of principles that we have constructed from the interview data. The principles operate within and through organizational structures and relationships and together define what we call 'the conditions of learning' (Rudduck *et al.*, 1996). They give weight and colour to the broad institutional frameworks or regimes that define what a pupil is, that determine the regularities of learning, and that, crucially, exert a powerful influence on young people's sense of purpose in learning and their pattern of achievement. According to the degree that they are present for each student they serve to construct different patterns of commitment and confidence. In a context where some students are advantaged and some disadvantaged by social background factors, the conditions of learning are an important factor in equalizing opportunity.

The six principles are not in themselves novel; indeed, they are likely to feature in most schools' statements of aims. What we have done is to come at them from the pupils' perspective and to reassert their central importance. The first three directly affect the student's 'sense of self-as-learner':

- *the principle of respect for students* as individuals and as a body occupying a significant position in the institution of the school;
- *the principle of fairness* to all students irrespective of their class, gender, ethnicity or academic status;
- *the principle of autonomy* (not as an absolute state but as both a right and a responsibility in relation to physical and social maturity).

The next three principles are more about what happens in and out of the classroom and suggest the importance of balancing risk-taking in school work with confidence about one's self and one's image:

- *the principle of intellectual challenge* that helps students to experience learning as a dynamic, engaging and empowering activity;
- *the principle of support* in relation to both academic and emotional concerns;
- *the principle of security* in relation to the physical setting of the school, in social interactions (especially pupils' anxieties about being taunted or mocked) and in relation to intellectual tasks (so that pupils feel confident about learning from mistakes and misunderstandings).

Figure 4 shows how it fits together:

Figure 4

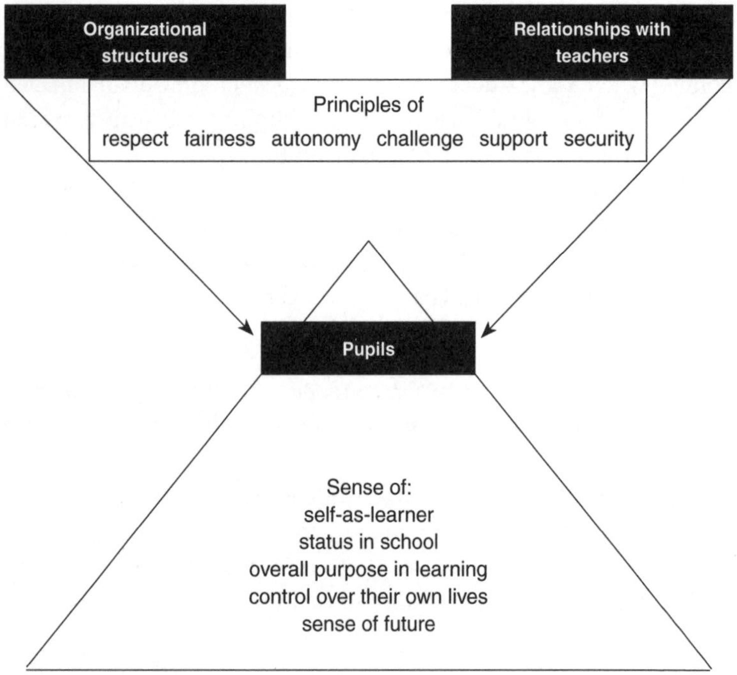

Organizational structures

Relationships with teachers

Principles of
respect   fairness   autonomy   challenge   support   security

Pupils

Sense of:
self-as-learner
status in school
overall purpose in learning
control over their own lives
sense of future

Some aspects of *organizational structures* are a powerful force in creating different patterns of opportunity and advantage. It is important to understand:

- how material and human resources are allocated to different groups of pupils and tasks and what priorities are reflected;
- how pupils are divided and labelled;
- how well schools explain the rationale for particular rules, regimes or new procedures;
- how rewards and sanctions are handled and how and to whom expectations of high achievement are communicated.

By *relationships* we mean the interactions, within school, of teachers and pupils (we are not here focusing on pupil–pupil interactions). Our interviews suggest that what we should be concerned about are the *messages* that such interactions communicate to pupils about themselves as learners. Certain kinds of interactions, or opportunities for interaction, are highlighted in the interviews as carrying strong positive tones – for instance:

- teachers being available to talk with pupils about learning and school work, not just about behaviour;
- teachers recognizing pupils' desire to take more responsibility as they grow older;
- teachers' readiness to engage with pupils in adult ways;
- teachers being sensitive to the tone and manner of their discourse with pupils, as individuals and in groups, so that they do not criticise them in ways that make them feel small (especially in front of their peers);
- teachers being seen to be fair in all their dealings with all pupils;
- teachers' acceptance, demonstrated in action, that an important aspect of fairness is not prejudging pupils on the basis of past incidents;
- teachers ensuring that they make *all* pupils feel confident that they can do well and can achieve something worthwhile.

We are talking here about the social conditions of learning but equally important are the pedagogic conditions of learning. We saw in Chapter 3 what pupils say about the kind of teacher and teaching that can capture and sustain their interest in learning.

*

This chapter has explored what factors influence our conception of the kind of pupil we want in school. It has also indicated how the conditions of learning in school can intervene to define, extend or limit that vision. Finally, it reminds us that in the context of pupil voice we need to put alongside the opening question, 'What kind of pupil do we want in school? another question, 'What kind of school do pupils want to be in?' The next chapter looks at the transformative potential of pupil voice and whether it can lead to *real* school improvement – i.e. improved conditions for learning in schools and not just improved test scores.

6 Pupil Voice And Schools: The Transformative Potential

> How youth find a voice in schools when schooling structures, policies and practices are so often crafted in such ways as to ensure that no voice is possible is a question worthy of examination. (Erickson and Schultz, 1992, p. 5)

In the intervening years since Erickson and Schultz wrote this there has been a lot of progress but in a relatively small number of schools. Despite the legitimation provided by the children's rights movement, the school improvement movement and citizenship education – and despite the encouraging models of good practice that these pioneering schools offer – for most of us, realizing the 'transformative potential' of pupil voice will still be difficult.

What does this rather grandiose term, 'the transformative potential', mean for teachers and schools? It is certainly not about 'quick fixes' and it is much more than mere 'tinkering'; these are metaphors from a system that is preoccupied with the attainment of prescribed goals rather than with the unpredictable achievements of its key members – its pupils and its teachers. At a general level 'transformation' is about root and branch change of perception and practice although the detail will, inevitably, be context dependent. As Mitchell and Sackney see it, transformation means moving from a technological model that is concerned with targets, efficiency and hierarchical modes of accountability to one that is characterized by 'metaphors of wholeness and connections, diversity and complexity, relationships and meaning, reflection and enquiry, and collaboration and collegiality' (2000, p. 6). They attribute the style of the former to a 'learning organization', the style of the latter to 'a learning community'.

In most schools, transformation will be about re-casting teachers and pupils in a more participatory and collaborative relationship, reviewing perceptions of pupils' capacities to contribute actively to a range of school activities, and allowing them to move outside their assigned cells as learners of the statutory curriculum into learnings associated with a wider range of roles and purposes. As the National Educational Research Forum said in one of its recent documents, 'mass education must change if it is to create the inquisitive, innovative and entrepreneurial' young people our society needs.

This view is widely echoed. For example, Larsen (2001, p. 69) argues that 'In thinking about a school for the 21st century ... the central concern must be on changing the way students and teachers engage with learning.' And Rachal (1998, p. 186) suggests that a 'schooling atmosphere' needs to give way to 'a less hierarchical and more collaborative relationship', and recalls Freire's (1970) idea of 'culture circles' in which the learners' voices and experiences are heard and valued.

A key moment in the process of transformation is when members of the school come to value critical reflection as a way of learning and are committed to building a climate of openness, trust and respect in which review can be used and experienced as a constructive process rather than as a top-down whiplash. Double-loop learning – which involves a readiness to examine the appropriateness of the present system and seek alternatives where there are deemed to be inadequacies – will be as, or more, important than the system-maintenance initiatives of single-loop thinking:

> [Change] begins with a confrontation with the values, assumptions, belief systems, and practices that individuals embrace. This is a profoundly personal and potentially transforming phenomenon. As educators come to grips with the implicit narratives that shape and constrain their professional practice and learning, they gain some sense of mastery over what they do know and what they need to know. This knowledge empowers them to begin a search for new knowledge and to reconstruct their professional narrative. (Mitchell and Sackney, 2000, p. 13)

This process needs to be supported not only at the level of teachers (the 'educators' in the quotation above) but also at the level of the pupil and the school as a whole. Confidence in the process builds up as groups and individuals begin to experience a sense of common purpose and shared responsibility:

> A learning community emerges as individuals reflect on, assess, critique and reconstruct their personal professional capacity and their capacity for collegial relations and collective practice. (*Ibid.*)

In short, a learning community is 'a place of reflection, inquiry, discourse sharing, and risk-taking, where its participants engage in these processes from a desire to learn and to seek better ways of doing things' (p. 133). School improvement is not, therefore, a question of a quick make-over to meet the requirements of the moment; it is not about rescuing the kids likely to get a D grade and using available resources to shore up their chances of getting C grades while giving scant support to the no-hopers. It is not about a bit of liposuction to improve the school's grades profile. It is, instead, about reviewing the deep structures and patterns of relationship in order to enable a school to move from a learning organization to a learning community.

What does pupil consultation mean for teachers?

In the present system teachers are the gatekeepers of change. It was Lawrence Stenhouse who said that only teachers could really 'change the world of the classroom' and that they would do so by first understanding it (1975, p. 208). But children's learning will never be understood properly if teachers cannot spend time listening to the children (Hall and Martello, 1996, p. vi).

Evidence from various projects we have worked on suggests that hearing what pupils have to say about teaching, learning and schooling enables teachers to look at things from the pupil perspective – and the world of school can look very different from this angle. Being prepared – and being able – to see the familiar differently and to contemplate alternative approaches, roles and practices is the first step towards fundamental change in classrooms and schools.

Teacher research is one productive arena for such shifts of perception. Teaching is vulnerable to the flattening effect of habit, and research can help teachers look behind what is taken for granted in everyday practice. Habit is seductive: it is soothing and compulsive. To get a research grip on a problem often requires that we see 'ordinary' events and interactions with new eyes, for significances become obscured by the familiarity of the everyday context. Our everyday eyes have two understandable weaknesses. First, because of the dominance of habit and routine, we are only selectively attentive to the phenomena of our classrooms. In a sense we are constantly reconstructing the world we are familiar with in order to maintain regularities and routines. Second, because of our busy-ness, our eyes tend only to transcribe the surface realities of classroom interaction. The aim in teacher research is, however, for the teacher to attain the eyes of the stranger or artist, for it is art that teaches the sensitivity of being attentive to significances that normally remain uncelebrated. As Seifert (1983, p. 56) has said:

> In the outlines of the things on which I look
> I paint what the eye does not see.
> And that is art.

Teachers need sometimes to abandon their habitual way of perceiving the world of school and classroom in order to be receptive to its problems. Once they see the seeds of a worthwhile problem then they must frame that problem, gather data, derive explanations and test those explanations. Here the art/science dichotomy is useful, for one might claim that art is a way of representing reality and science is a way of explaining that same reality (Read, 1958). Both are central aspects of classroom-based research. What an art critic (Bryson, 1990) wrote about the underrated genre of still life painting rings true for the overlooked potential of the student perspective: 'the worldly scale of importance is deliberately assaulted by plunging attention downwards ... the eye's enslavement to the world's ideas of what is worthy of attention [is challenged]' and attention itself gains power in the process.

However, a weakness of teacher research, as it has become more popular and been increasingly championed by government or quasi-government agencies, is that it has tended to lose its teeth – it 'neither threatens nor is itself threatened', as Adelman and Carr (1988) put it. It sometimes addresses easy questions that have no leverage for fundamental change within the school as a community. It is rarely cumulative in the sense that it builds on other reported research in the field – although a more telling issue is whether teacher research is cumulative *within* the school, contributing towards a new coherence of perception and practice. Indeed, the distinctive image of teacher research – the individual struggling to understand the events and situations of his or her own classroom – may not be a powerful force for change unless it is framed by an emerging sense of the school as a community of practice (Eckert *et al.*, 1996, pp. 4–5; in Holloway and Valentine, 2003, p. 14).

In-service education is another source of support in enabling the teacher to step outside the everyday circle of requirements and expectations and to look in with the temporary eyes of a stranger. But the potential of externally led in-service activities to 'build and sustain alternative habits of thought and disposition' (see Rudduck, 1991, p. 135) will not be realized unless it encourages 'teachers to reflect critically on their own educational views and on the nature of education as it is realised in the institutional setting of schools …' (Carr, 1986, p. 6).

The third way – and all three may be needed! – is to elicit and engage with the perspectives of the pupils in one's own classroom and school. Across various projects developed in partnership with teachers we have built up a body of evidence that demonstrates the power of pupil voice to enable teachers to change their perception of pupils' capabilities and, consequently, to change their practices and ways of relating. Donald Schon, way back in 1983 when *The Reflective Practitioner* was published, said this:

> A professional practitioner is a specialist who encounters certain types of situation again and again … [but] many practitioners, locked into a view of themselves as technical experts, find nothing in the world of practice to occasion reflection. (p. 69)

For many teachers, hearing their pupils talk about teaching and learning can be such a catalyst. This teacher records her surprise at the power of pupils' comments:

You know – that's what made me enthusiastic, because I suddenly saw all that untapped creativity really ... You can use pupils' ideas in a very valid, interesting way and it can make the pupil excited, the teacher excited and you know obviously the lessons will take off from there. It's like going on a teachers' conference and sort of thinking, 'Oh, that's a good idea' and planning a series of lessons together. You know ... although you do a bit of collaborating together with other teachers, there's not that much time any more, so, you know, if you can actually collaborate with pupils it's equally – I didn't realise it – it's equally exciting, isn't it? (McIntyre and Pedder, in press)

The teachers quoted below who contributed to the ESRC/TLRP *Consulting Pupils Project*, comment on how pupils have changed as a result of being consulted and also how they themselves have changed aspects of their teaching in response to what pupils have said:

We've learned a lot ... about how students rapidly improve in their learning and their self-esteem and their motivation through dialogue with staff, through feeling important, feeling cared for, feeling their views matter. I think it's had a really, really significant effect.

We've had some very clear pointers from students about how they like to learn and I think it's given quite an encouragement to different ways of teaching ... We've modified things or developed things further – and had the courage of our convictions.

We've learnt a lot about targets: how overwhelming targets can be if you set 33, you know, because every member of staff has to set three or four. We've changed our policy as a result. (MacBeath *et al.*, 2003)

Teachers also say how their perceptions of pupils' capabilities have changed as a result of talking with them about some of the taken-for-granted aspects of teaching and learning. They report a much more positive view of pupils' capacities for observation and constructive analysis:

I know I shouldn't be [but] I'm still astounded at the depth of their honesty. And about how much if we listen we can learn and influence what's happening with them and be part of what's happening with them. (Macbeath *et al.*, 2003)

Another teacher, from a different pupil voice project (Newman, 1997, pp. 10–12), said this: 'I find they say things that I would not necessarily have thought of because of my own preconceptions'; and again, 'Children's responses are really surprising ... you don't know what goes on in their heads.' Researchers' observations echo such comments:

> What surprised us most about the pupils was how insightful they were and how fluent many were ... at expressing their ideas. What surprised *them* most was that anybody was prepared to listen. (Osborne and Collins, 2000)

One outcome for some teachers is a determination to set a broader frame for the valuing of pupils' achievement which might include such things as their capacity to analyse social situations, their skill in supporting their peers, their contribution to collaborative planning and decision-making, their capacity to look at situations from different perspectives – all things that seem to be strengthened through the experience of greater consultation and participation. But although the potential outcomes are clear, the undergrowth is full of snares. Teachers who stand on the edge of consulting pupils, interested but uncertain whether to proceed, talk mainly about the problem of time but there are also deeper concerns – for instance, about the possibility of personal criticism and about the loss of a familiar power base.

The issue of time

Time is an issue in its own right but it also links to dilemmas about priorities. Consulting pupils is appealing because, as we have suggested earlier, it restores to centre stage the key professional relationship of teacher, pupils and learning. It is professionally recreative to tune in to students rather than to policy makers. But teachers see the National Curriculum and the government's preoccupation with targets as offering little freedom for manoeuvre and the thought of 'providing all students with a chance to negotiate, plan for and participate' can be daunting, especially when added to 'an already overcrowded curriculum and to the planning burden of already overstretched teachers' (Jerome, 2001, p. 9). It is not a task for the faint-hearted.

Committing yourself to exploring the potential of pupil voice is also intellectually disturbing. If teachers have resigned themselves to working for the narrow attainment targets set by the government and helping their school run the race in the national comparison stakes, then strategies that ask some fundamental questions about pupils and schools today will disturb the already uneasy equilibrium.

Such tensions are not new – although they take different forms at different periods. For A. S. Neill, in his pre-Summerhill days, they presented themselves as a choice between education as a way of life and training for a job: 'I want to teach my bairns how to live; the Popular Education wants to teach them how to make a living. There is a distinction between the two ideals' (1917, p. 46). And for Lawrence Stenhouse the clash was between two interpretations of standards: the external view then, as now, was of standards as yardsticks for judging winners and losers which operated in ways that reduced pupils to 'standard deviations' (1979, p. 75). His own view was that standards were the criteria by which a working group of teacher and students decided to judge the way they worked together and to value their individual and collective achievements (1964; 1983, p. 49).

There is, in the present climate, some security in the idea of moving towards familiar goals in familiar ways, but many teachers are nonetheless ready to trade in the quieter life for more risk and excitement and a better deal for their students. Many recognize and are impatient with what Frowe calls 'the commodification of education', and its modernizing vocabulary of 'delivery', 'consumers', 'markets', and 'output characteristics'. As Frowe says, the language 'is not simply a passive record keeper but an active constituent of the practice' and its effect could be profoundly dehumanizing and mechanizing: 'there is little time for genuinely open conversations through which children may have opportunities to develop their understanding and learning' (2001, pp. 95; 96; 98).

A focus on pupils requires an active response and teachers may want to confront and explore some of the contradictions in the system – the narrow perspective of performativity on the one hand and the broader, more inclusive perspective that underpins pupil voice on the other. Of course, as we know from decades of externally led curriculum development, teachers have ways, in the privacy of their own classrooms and departments, of quietly subverting requirements that they disagree with; however they may now feel more profoundly angry at being 'simply the tools by which other people's agendas and wishes are enacted' (Mitchell and Sackney, 2000, p. 128) and they may be ready to reassert their own professional autonomy. Sergiovanni also puts teachers in the central – and pivotal – position:

> Teachers count in helping schools to be effective. But whether they will help students in a particular school or not depends on whether they are invested with enough discretion to act ... Building capacity among teachers and focusing that capacity on students and their learning is the crucial factor. Continuous capacity building and continuous focusing is best done within communities of practice. (Sergiovanni, 2000, p. 140; in Mitchell and Sackney, 2000, p. 11)

We see teachers as the 'professional creators' of a new culture of learning. Listening to pupils, developing a stronger collaboration with them, and all that this entails, will help teachers to develop what Bredeson (1999, p. 22) calls a 'critical competence' – that is, a capacity, as a staff, to look analytically and constructively at school practices and structures. Such a competence is the precondition for Sergiovanni's process of continuous focusing and re-focusing which is the key to informed change.

The issue of fear and anxiety

Engaging in pupil consultation presents, for teachers, some potentially uncomfortable prospects: in particular, concern about being on the receiving end of personal criticism, and concern about what happens if the familiar hierarchical structure of the classroom is challenged by the principle of partnership.

Anxiety is an understandable response:

> For most individuals in any organization, the challenge of fear and anxiety is always at least in the back of their minds if not front and centre. People often feel vulnerable, unsafe, and inadequate when trust is not present. Furthermore, all learning involves risks and therefore some fear. (Mitchell and Sackney, 2001, p. 107)

Senge *et al.* (1999, pp. 244–50, in Mitchell and Sackney, 2000, p. 107) suggest some strategies for responding to evidence of unease among colleagues:

- reminding people that fear and anxiety are natural responses;
- starting small and building momentum before confronting difficult issues;
- avoiding full frontal oppositional assaults;
- ensuring that participation is a matter of choice and not coercion.

Fear and anxiety can be also be allayed by hearing accounts from teachers in other classrooms or schools who have tried giving pupils a voice, who have survived the experience and become excited by the possibilities it opens up:

> Staff that you thought wouldn't ever listen who'd say, 'Fine, yes, but that's not for me' – once they see the students reacting and hear what they're saying (and they may be saying in a lesson, 'Well would you mind if I did that a slightly different way, would that be all right?') they're suddenly thinking, 'Well, maybe they *do* know what they're talking about'. And that brings more staff in. (Mullis, 2002)

There will be some settings where, because of the sharpness of the 'them and us' divide, the accounts given by pupils to outside researchers – they are unlikely to talk openly at first to their own teachers – may be harsh. Severe criticism of school regimes is often triggered by perceptions of the different ways in which different groups are treated, valued and privileged but if schools are to improve, this is the kind of uncomfortable self-knowledge that they need to confront. However, the problem can lie the other way round: pupils are perhaps too accepting of the status quo and their position in it:

> Students' wishes today are modest, even timid. They do not seek to overthrow the system or even to control it. They expect and want educators to remain in control. They do, however, want to understand why things are done as they are. They would like to be able to voice their views about change and have them heard. They wish to have some choice about how and what they learn. On the whole they are amazingly accepting of the standard organisation and practices of schools. (Levin, 1999)

For example, an adolescent boy who finds learning a struggle in his school accepts the division that is implicit, and sometimes explicit, in the messages he receives every day – and which he repeats with a resigned authority: 'Them what's thick's thick and them what's brainy's brainy.' Such resignation is, of course, also protective of the energy needed to change things; this is 'reflexive conservatism' at the level of the pupil. Prout and James suggest, citing Foucault, that these institutional 'discourse circles' are difficult to crack open; they

> operate rather like self-fulfilling prophecies: ways of thinking about childhood fuse with institutionalized practices to produce self-conscious subjects … who think (and feel) about themselves through the terms of these ways of thinking. 'The truth' about themselves and their situation is thus self-validating. Breaking into this with another 'truth' (produced by another way of thinking about childhood) may prove difficult. (1997, p. 23)

Pupils' identities as learners are often constructed by the prevailing discourse of differentiation and division and sometimes, too, of derision.

As we said at the start of this section, we see teachers as the gate-keepers of change, as the people who hold the keys to transformation, but it is not an easy journey. Transformation involves rethinking professional identities and relationships with pupils – and both of these have served as anchors in successive waves of government-led initiatives rather than as obvious arenas for change.

What does pupil consultation mean for schools?

Schools, in their deep structures and regimes, can seem as imper-meable as tanks – built to resist onslaught from the outside. Despite many sequences of change efforts (see Goodlad, 1984) schools remain, in broad outline, much as they were. As Maxine Greene said (1985): they 'seem to resemble natural processes: what goes on in them appears to have the sanction of natural law and can no more be questioned and resisted than the law of gravity'.

Achieving change in the basic conditions of learning in schools, as Watson and Fullan (1992) have said, '… will not happen by accident, good will or … *ad hoc* projects. It requires new structures, new activities, and a rethinking of the internal workings of each institution'. Schools will need support in the task of 'reshaping long-standing structures that have fostered disconnection, separateness, division' – features that have prevented teachers and students in schools from 'sharing powerful ideas about how to make schools better' (Warsley *et al.*, 1997, p. 204).

Part of the problem is the change process itself. Philip Runkel observed, some years ago, that an innovative school is one that tries one thing after another without getting any of them to work (1984, p. 178). More recently Tyack and Tobin (1990, p. 465) have reminded us about the temptation of the project conveyor belt: 'Each is taken up in turn ... elbowed out to make room for the next newcomer, and yet we are not saved.' At the moment, the sequencing of the conveyor belt has given way to simultaneous change efforts and there is a temptation for schools to become involved in numerous initiatives, each offering small amounts of money and/or a certain prestige. It is rather like letting loose a flight of arrows, each with a different substance/message which, if they do penetrate the institutional skin, do not singly have the power to spread beyond the particular entry point of the receiving teacher's mindset and classroom. But if the arrows all carried the same message, the impact on the institutional body could be powerful. The discipline and economy of building whole-school coherence around key issues and values is surely the best way forward.

A recent study tells the story of how one school in very difficult circumstances achieved 'success against the odds' but it took time and patience. It was not about rapid turnarounds and 'miracle gro' headteachers; it was a story of commitment to a core set of values which, when the climate changed and the going became tough, held the staff together like the rope that links a team of mountaineers on an icy cliff face. These were some of the understandings that emerged from the study of the Sutton Centre School (Rudduck and Morrison, 2002, pp. 303–4):

- Coherence is more likely to be achieved when policies and their daily enactment in practice are consistently informed by a clearly defined set of principles and values.

- External requirements can sometimes be acted on in ways that serve the principles and values that the school holds dear; in this way the intensification of work that they represent can become more acceptable.
- Improvement will be a slow process when changing the culture (or 'ways of seeing') of members of the school or the community is a condition of progress.
- Sometimes, for schools that work in difficult circumstances, *sustaining* progress at the new level may itself be an achievement – requiring constant vigilance and energy. (Each new cohort of pupils can bring new challenges but cumulative experience of dealing with the problems enables more robust and reliable strategies to be developed.)
- Despite the 'ever onwards, ever upwards' motto of policy makers, schools may need to pace themselves. (Meteoric rises are what meteors do – and meteors burn out pretty quickly. As the head teacher said, 'The bedrock of our progress is the centrality of unspectacular, unmeteoric and unremitting graft'.)

What worries us about pupil consultation is that it is currently so high profile; high profile processes tend to be accompanied by expectations of observable improvement and clear-cut impact. But, as Fielding (2002a) says, the term 'impact' 'valorises what is short term, readily visible and easily measurable'. What the study of Sutton Centre reveals is the importance of a steady, sustained commitment to principles and values which will help a school to navigate the stormy waters of local and national debate about success and failure. Commitment was transformed into effective action by the staff's capacity for developing institutional self-knowledge over time. Freeman says that the important questions in school transformation are about the nature of collegiality: 'What is collegiality? It's difficult to spell, hard to pronounce, harder to define. It's hardest still to establish in a school' (2001). A sense of collegiality and common purpose proved to be an extremely important dimension of Sutton Centre's profile.

But what does all this mean for pupil voice? Hearing what students have to say about teaching and learning can offer *teachers* – as we said earlier:

- a more open perception of young people's capabilities;
- the capacity to see the familiar from a different angle;
- a readiness to change thinking and practice in the light of these perceptions;
- a renewed sense of excitement in teaching;
- a practical agenda for improvement.

What does it offer schools? The transformative potential relates most closely to the development of a stronger sense of the school as an inclusive community.

The potential will not be fully realized – and certainly not sustained – if it does not reach out beyond the individual teacher, however committed he or she may be, to the school. Too often in the history of innovation and change in school the initiative has remained the province of one teacher or one department where it has functioned as a cultural island, set apart from and having no interaction with mainstream values and practices in the school. As Louis and Miles remind us (1990, p. 5), the difficult part is 'getting new practices and ideas into the real life of the school'. As we saw in the story of Sutton Centre, shared understanding of, and a real commitment to, core values is a key to cultural change. And while collegiality is often thought about in relation to teachers (McGregor, 2002), our concern is with a notion of collegiality that is, in some sense, inclusive of pupils.

There is a difference, we think, between the potential impact of work on pupil perspectives and work on pupil voice. Teachers who are interested in pupil *perspectives*, as opposed to voice, may see pupils merely as sources of interesting and usable data but they are less likely to have goals that are expressed in terms of community. Eliciting and using pupil perspectives can usefully provide a practical agenda for change but it does not guarantee change in the status of pupils within the school. On the other hand, teachers concerned with *voice* usually take on the serious and significant task of eliciting and presenting the experiences and views of groups on the margins, thereby helping them to move from silence and invisibility to influence and visibility. Such work has a more transformative agenda (see Fielding, 1997) in that it implies a deeper review of pupils' roles and status in schools, at various levels and in various arenas.

One arena which richly repays investigation by looking at it from the pupils' perspective is language; another is space-and-place.

Space-and-place

Holloway and Valentine (2003, p. 48) point out that while *public* areas (such as parks and playgrounds) have been the focus of geographical studies of children's access to and use of space, only recently has the research moved into an analysis of space in schools. Many initiatives to do with children in public areas have been motivated by concerns about safety, and, as the authors point out (following Jackson and Scott, 1999, pp. 86–7), are about controlling the boundaries of movement as well as, incidentally, the boundaries of conceptions of childhood. They argue that it is important to look at the everyday spaces 'in, and through which, children's identities and lives are produced and reproduced' (2003, p. 6).

Pupils can feel that there are few areas which they have ownership of and where behaviours are not overly constrained by rules devised by adults. Having a home base which each year group can call its own is important to them, especially in schools where students are peripatetic and carry bags and baggage around from lesson to lesson. Gill Mullis, a secondary teacher, has highlighted the lack of areas in schools where her students-as-researchers group could meet to discuss their work and she records the consternation caused, initially, when the student secretary of the group tried to book the 'seminar room' – 'The seminar room is staff territory; it's a meeting room where normally students don't go' (Mullis, 2002). In order to break the habitual assumptions she adopted a strong 'That's what we do here' approach, and the school secretary who managed the room bookings gradually came to accept that students might also need a room to meet for discussions and were 'authorized agents' who could be trusted to make the booking themselves. Gill Mullis added, 'It's been two years now since anyone said to me, "Why are the students in the seminar room?"'

In this context we can recall several stories from different research projects. In an ethnographic study of an early years classroom, Clem Adelman disguised himself and his camera in a moving Dalek-type object called 'Charlie'; his filming of the everyday interactions of the classroom showed how the teacher's map of which territories and acts were *verboten* was not directly disclosed to pupils who learned by rebuke and punishment that they could not enter certain spaces or play with certain objects, such as the daffodils in the vases. In another incident, a primary school located in Victorian buildings, where each class had its own room and pupils their own desks, moved into new open-plan buildings without individual desk spaces. The insecurity that this move generated led some pupils, so the teachers thought, to steal pencils and rubbers and to hide them in little personal caches – in this way they were re-creating their *own* spaces and 'belongings'. In neither case had teachers tried to see the situation from the pupils' perspective and they had not therefore anticipated the likely responses. In their own small way these pupils were confirming the view of Mitchell and Sackney (2000, p. 3) that people are engaged constantly in the search for identity, companionship, sense of belonging – but also in the search for place.

In a third episode a primary school headteacher asked some of her younger pupils to walk her round the school and the classrooms and to show her things that helped them to learn and things that got in the way of their learning. She was surprised to find how the pupils responded to what she thought was a wonderful classroom display, with objects hanging down from the ceiling and projecting from the walls. But pupils said they kept on bumping into them and that they were a nuisance – but that their teacher liked them! And finally, when working on small group teaching in higher education (see Rudduck, 1978) one of us recalled advising lecturers to hold one-to-one seminars or supervisions in a neutral space rather than in their own rooms where messages about their power and status were apparent in many ways: in the stylistic or spatial relationship of their chair to the student's chair, in the plethora of personal objects that surrounded them, and where conversation might be interrupted by phone calls for the tutor but not for the student (in the age of mobile phones the balance of power in relation to phones may, of course, have changed!). As McGregor says (2002), time and again, 'space is mobilised as a resource in the production and reproduction of power relations between … teachers and students'.

In short, as schools seek to develop more inclusive communities, the issue of space and place needs to be on the agenda for review.

Language

In higher education, seminars are, in part, an occasion where students can learn to express and explore perspectives in ways that are appropriate within the discipline – where standards and boundaries are renewed and safeguarded by academics. Discussions function as a form of induction into the discourse style of the discipline. In schools, the language issue is more complex and is potentially more divisive. According to Gerald Grace, 'discourses are about what can be said and thought but also about who can speak, when, where and with what authority' (1995, p. 26). In short, discourses carry implicit messages about membership. Those whose language skills are closest to those valorized by the school are likely to feel a stronger sense of membership: 'Discourses embody meaning and social relationships, they constitute both subjectivity and power relations' (Grace, 1995, p. 26). Echoing Grace, and drawing on Bernstein's work, Reay and Arnot also ask whose voice gets heard in the acoustic of the school but they go further to show how language can reaffirm existing divisions in the school which, ironically, pupil voice initiatives are often designed to diminish.

For example, Mitra (2001) discusses the attempts of an ethnically and socially mixed group of students trying to work together on projects designed to enhance student responsibility and status in school:

> When the group first came together as a community of practice, they didn't yet have the language to articulate who they were. And this contributed to their struggles to agree upon a joint enterprise ... The students needed to get along with students different than them – students from different cliques, who speak different languages, who are different tracks in the school's academic system. (Mitra, 2001)

One of the problems was the feeling among some that those who were more articulate in the language of the school establishment were more likely to shape the decisions of the group, leaving others feeling disenfranchised in an initiative specifically designed to empower them. Silva discusses a similar problem (2001). One of the members of the student reform group, an African-American male, describes two broad types of student in the school – and, as it turned out, in the project group:

We've got squeaky wheels and flat tyres ... Some smooth white wheels rollin' their way right up to college, getting' oil all the way. And then the rest of us ... Flat tires! Bumpin' on down the road ... probably fall off real soon anyway. Ain't worth the grease. (Silva, 2001)

Problems in the group's working together again centred on language. The group

had to be diverse in order to work but the white female students at school had different views and a different language from black students who had experienced marginalisation. The latter wanted the group to be challenging and activist ... In comparison, the successful students, predominantly white, expected the group to be less reformist. (Silva, 2001)

The important point is that consultation processes can sometimes reflect or re-enforce rather than challenge the existing dividing practices in schools and the regimes which lead to some pupils being valued above others.

Indeed, we have some evidence that teachers who are working in traditional school cultures are starting to build their new 'learning community' by working in a small-scale and relatively protected way with a few students. These students are then invited to 'display' their capacities for constructive analytic dialogue to other teachers, to the senior management team and sometimes to governors and to conferences of pupils and teachers in other settings. By and large the reports show how readily the students (particularly, perhaps, the girls) develop a command of the situation, meeting the different challenges with maturity and confidence. But the problem is that these pioneering groups of students can become an elite, creating new hierarchies within the body of students itself – and their status is often rooted in competence in talk which may, in turn, be linked to social class.

There are some other language-linked issues. In the flatter hierarchies and more distributive power structures of some schools, discussions between teachers and pupils are an important outcome of the strengthening of collegial relationships. But we need to be attentive to the existence of divergent voices in the group: for example, after a class or school referendum has been organized and analysed it is important that there is feedback to the students whose views have been canvassed and that space is made for discussion of what actions can be pursued from among those suggested; minority positions need to be noted and respected and not merely dismissed out of hand in favour of what might be a comfortable and somewhat conservative consensus of the articulate majority.

And, again, as Fielding has said (2002), we have to ask whether the topics 'permitted' for discussion in schools are ones that *pupils* see as significant and whether the discussions are occasions for genuine dialogue in which students can speak, without fear of retaliation, of 'concerns, passions and interests which are rooted in their developing sense of justice and of self'. He went on: initiatives that seek student opinion on matters identified, framed and articulated by researchers or teachers, or that invite comment on issues that students see as important and that do not lead to recognizable action – or discussion of possible courses of action – are unlikely to be seen as credible. Students will soon tire of invitations (a) to express a view on matters they do not think are important, (b) that are framed in a language they find restrictive, alienating or patronizing, and (c) that seldom result in actions or dialogue that affects the quality of their lives. Fielding concluded: 'We ... regard it as crucial for student perceptions and recommendations to be responded to, not merely treated as minor footnotes in an unaltered adult text.'

*

This chapter suggests that the transformative potential of consulting pupils is considerable but that it can fall short of making a difference to and for students because of power issues embedded in the everyday regimes of schools and even woven into the very strategies we use for consulting pupils. The chapter has tried, however, to demonstrate how consultation can help build a more inclusive ethos in schools and it identifies some arenas (space-and-place and language) where principles of inclusion are particularly vulnerable. Finally, it argues that an innovation, to realize its transformative potential, needs to move from being the province or test bed of one or more teachers to take on a 'community commitment' at the level of the whole school.

Despite the contradictory imperatives of performance goals, national policy *is* supportive of pupil voice initiatives and the idea of consulting pupils *is* making its way into teachers' practices and school policies up and down the country. It is important to seize the moment so that more of us in education, for the sake of our pupils, will be able to share Raymond Williams's 'passionate concern that people who might otherwise find themselves victims of history' should be able instead to understand and take some control over their own circumstances (Hare, 1989). That, ultimately, is what the transformative potential of pupil voice is all about.

Appendix: Information On The Contributing Projects

Making Your Way Through Secondary School

Funded by: ESRC, 1991–4.

Focus: Pupils' perceptions of learning and of themselves as learners as they moved through the final four years of compulsory secondary schooling. Eighty pupils were involved from three schools in three LEAs; in all we built up a data set of over 800 transcribed pupil and teacher interviews.

Team members: Julia Flutter, David Gillborn, Susan Harris, Jean Rudduck and Gwen Wallace.

Main outputs

Harris, S. and Rudduck, J. (1993) 'Establishing the seriousness of learning', *British Journal of Educational Psychology*, Vol. 63 (part 2), 322–66.

Harris, S., Rudduck, J. and Wallace, G. (1994) '"School's great – apart from the lessons": students' early experiences of learning in secondary school', in M. Hughes (ed.) *Perceptions of Teaching and Learning*, Clevedon: Multilingual Matters, pp. 35–52.

Harris, S., Wallace, G. and Rudduck, J. (1995) '"It's not that I haven't learnt much. It's just that I don't really know what I'm doing": metacognition and secondary school students', *Research Papers in Education*, 10, 2, 134–53.

Rudduck, J., Chaplain, R., and Wallace, G. (1996) *School Improvement: What Can Pupils Tell Us?*, London: David Fulton.

Rudduck, J., Day, J. and Wallace, G. (1996) 'The significance for school improvement of pupils' experiences of within-school transitions', *Curriculum*, 17, 3, 144–53.

Rudduck, J., Wallace, G. and Day, J. (2000) 'Students' voices: what can they tell us as partners in change?', in K. Stott and V. Trafford (eds) *Partnerships: Shaping the Future of Education*, London: Middlesex University Press, pp. 1–26.

Thinking about Learning, Talking about Learning

Funded by: Cambridgeshire LEA; phase 1, 1997–8; phase 2, 1998–9.

Focus: Classroom-based teacher-research studies exploring, in different contexts, what we can learn from pupils about three topics: what makes a piece of work 'good'; what gets in the way of working hard; and what makes learning exciting. Sixteen schools (infants, primary, secondary and special schools) were involved in phase 1 and another 14 were involved in phase 2.

Team members: Julia Flutter, Ruth Kershner and Jean Rudduck, together with LEA advisers; other colleagues from Homerton College were involved in supporting the work of individual schools. (Note: the two peer mentoring projects described in Chapter 2 were part of phase 2.)

Main outputs

Flutter, J., Kershner, R. and Rudduck, J. (1998) *The Effective Learning Project*, Cambridge: Cambridgeshire LEA.

Morrison, I., Everton, T. and Rudduck, J. (2000) 'Pupils helping other pupils with their learning: cross-age tutoring in a primary and secondary school', *Mentoring and Tutoring*, 8, 3, 187–200.

Giving Year 8 a Positive Identity

Funded by: Lincolnshire LEA, 1997–8.

Focus: An exploration, from the pupil perspective, of the 'dip' in progress in Year 8, which Ofsted identified, and possible ways of giving Year 8 a more positive identity. Nine secondary schools were involved. (Note: the Year 8 mentoring initiative described in Chapter 2 was part of this project.)

Team members: Julia Flutter, Jean Rudduck and Elaine Wilson.

Main outputs

Rudduck, J. Wilson, E. and Flutter, J. (1998) *Sustaining Pupils' Commitment to Learning: The Challenge of Year 8*, Cambridge: Homerton Publications.

Doddington, C., Flutter, J. and Rudduck, J. (1998) 'Year 8 – a suitable case for treatment', *Improving Schools*, 1, 3, 39–42.

Batty, J., Rudduck, J. and Wilson, E. (1999) 'What makes a good mentor? Who makes a good mentor? The views of Year 8 mentees', *Educational Action Research*, 7, 3, 365–74.

Improving Learning: The Pupils' Agenda

Funded by: The Nuffield Foundation, 1997–8.

Focus: Two parallel projects, one working with primary and the other with secondary schools; in all 46 schools across the country were involved. Three issues were explored: pupils helping other pupils with their learning; catching up and keeping up; and creating a positive learning environment.

Team members: Primary team: Chris Doddington, Julia Flutter and Jean Rudduck; secondary team: Julia Flutter and Jean Rudduck from Cambridge; Helen Addams, Michael Johnson and Margaret Maden from Keele.

Main outputs

Doddington, C., Flutter, J. and Rudduck, J. (1999) *Improving Learning: The Pupils' Agenda (a report for primary schools)*, Cambridge: Homerton Research Unit.

Flutter, J., Rudduck, J., Addams, H., Johnson, M. and Maden, M. (1999) *Improving Learning: The Pupils' Agenda* (a report for secondary schools), Cambridge: Homerton Research Unit.

Sustaining Pupils' Progress at Year 3

Funded by: Ofsted, 1999–2000.

Focus: Teachers' and pupils' perceptions of the transition from Year 2 to Year 3 and the implications for pupils' progress. Sixteen schools were involved from two LEAs.

Team members: Chris Doddington, Julia Flutter, Eve Bearne and Helen Demetriou.

Main outputs

Bearne, E. 'A good listening to: Year 3 pupils talk about their learning', *Support for Learning*, 17, 3.

Doddington, C. and Flutter, J. with Bearne, E. and Demetriou, H. (2001) *Sustaining Pupils' Progress at Year 3*, Cambridge: Faculty of Education Publication.

Doddington, C., Flutter, J. and Rudduck, J. (1999) 'Exploring and explaining "dips" in motivation and performance in primary and secondary schooling', *Research in Education*, 61, 29–38.

Learning About Improvement (the LAiMP Project)

Funded by: West Sussex LEA, phase 1, 1998–9; phase 2, 2000–1 (the work in each phase spanned five terms).

Focus: Both phases had two distinctive concerns: to support teachers in working with and learning from other schools; to support schools in exploring the potential of consulting students about teaching, learning and schooling. In all, 20 secondary schools and one middle school were involved.

Team members: Phase 1: Jean Rudduck, Mary Berry, Nick Brown and David Frost; phase 2: Mary Berry, Nick Brown, Lesley Hendy and Jean Rudduck.

Main outputs

Rudduck, J., Berry, M., Brown, N. and Hendy, L. (2003) with Chandler, M., Enright, P. and Godly, J. (2003) 'Learning about improvement by talking about improvement', *Improving Schools*, 5, 3, 34–45.

Rudduck, J., Berry, M., Frost, D. with Brown, N. (2000) 'Learning from other schools in a climate of competition', *Research Papers in Education*, 15, 3, 259–74.

Rudduck, J., Berry, M., Frost, D. and Brown, N. (2000) *Learning from Other Schools in a Climate of Competition*, Project Report, West Sussex County Council.

The Transfer and Transitions Project

This project had three strands (led by Maurice Galton, John Gray and Jean Rudduck). The third, which looked at personal and institutional transitions, consisted of three small-scale research and development projects, one on friendships post-transfer, another on supporting pupils in the transition from 'dosser' to 'worker', and the third on within-school transitions and the importance of giving each year a strong learning-oriented identity.

Friendships and Performance at Transfer and Beyond

Funded by: DfES as part of its broader project on transfer, transition and pupil progress, 2000–3.

Focus: Teachers' and pupils' perceptions of how friends contribute or get in the way of pupils' commitment to learning; 14 primary and secondary schools were involved in the pilot phase, and 5 secondary schools in the development phase.

Team members: Helen Demetriou, Paul Goalen and Jean Rudduck.

Supporting pupils in re-tracking

Funded by: DfES as part of its broader project on transfer, transition and pupil progress, 2000–3.

Focus: Understanding why pupils switch off and how they can be helped to make the personal transition from 'shirker' to 'worker'; 7 secondary schools were involved in the development phase.

Team members: Mary Berry and Jean Rudduck.

Transitions in the secondary school

Funded by: DfES as part of its broader project on transfer, transition and pupil progress, 2000–3.

Focus: Building on earlier work on pupils' perceptions of Year 8, this project looked at induction and other events for Years 8 and 10.

Team members: Mary Berry and Jean Rudduck.

Main outputs across the three projects

Demetriou, H., Goalen, P. and Rudduck, J. (2000) 'Academic performance, transfer, transition and friendship: listening to the student voice', *International Journal of Educational Research*, 33, 425–41.

Galton, M., Gray, J. and Rudduck, J. (2003) *Progress in the Middle Years of Schooling (7–14): Continuities and Discontinuities in Learning*; London: HMSO.

Consulting Pupils about Teaching and Learning

Funded by: ESRC in phase 1 of its Teaching and Learning Research Programme (TLRP); the project started in January 2001 and ended in December 2003.

Focus: The project had a number of interlocking themes: ways of consulting pupils about teaching and learning; what pupils can tell us about the social conditions of learning in the classroom; what teachers learn from pupil consultation and what they make use of; developing consultation as a whole-school strategy; the relationship between pupil consultation, engagement and learning; students as researchers. The project also supported teachers in schools across the country in developing consultation projects in their own classrooms.

Team members: Madeleine Arnot, Sara Bragg, Nick Brown, Nichola Daily (secretary), Helen Demetriou, Michael Fielding, Julia Flutter, John MacBeath, Donald McIntyre, Kate Myers, Dave Pedder, Diane Reay, Jean Rudduck (co-ordinator), Beth Wang.

Main outputs

Arnot, M., McIntyre, D., Pedder, D. and Reay, D. (2003) *Consultation in the Classroom: Developing Dialogue about Teaching and Learning*, Cambridge: Pearson Publishing.

Bragg, S. (2001) 'Taking a joke: learning from the voices we don't want to hear', *Forum*, 43, 2, 70–3.

Fielding, M. and Bragg, S. (2003) *Students as Researchers: Making a Difference*, Cambridge: Pearson Publishing.

Fielding, M. (2001) 'Beyond the rhetoric of student voice: new departures or new constraints in the transformation of 21st-century schooling', *Forum*, 43, 2, 100–9.

Fielding, M. (ed.) (2001) Special edition on pupil voice, *Forum*, 43, 2.

Flutter, J. and Rudduck, J. (2004) *Consulting Pupils: What's In it for Schools?* London: Routledge Falmer.

MacBeath, J., Demetriou, H., Rudduck, J. and Myers, K. (2003), *Consulting Pupils: A Toolkit for Teachers*, Cambridge: Pearson Publishing.

MacBeath, J., Myers, K. and Demetriou, H. (2001) 'Supporting teachers in consulting pupils about aspects of teaching and learning', *Forum*, 43, 2, 78–82.

Rudduck, J. (2001) 'Students and school improvement: "Transcending the cramped conditions of the time"', *Improving Schools*, 4, 2, 7–16.

Rudduck, J. (in press) 'The transformative potential of consulting young people about teaching, learning and schooling', *Scottish Educational Review*.

Rudduck, J. and Demetriou, H. with Pedder, D. (2003) 'Student perspectives and teacher practices: the transformative potential', *McGill Journal of Education*, 38, 2, 274–88.

Note

Some quotations in the text are referenced as fieldwork data:

Nick Brown's fieldwork data: the quotations are from either the *Learning about Improvement Project* (see above) or the *Consulting Pupils about Teaching and Learning* Project (see above).

Mary Earl's fieldwork data: the quotations are from a small-scale study of Year 10 and Year 11 students' attitudes to RE.

Susan Harris's fieldwork data: the quotations are from data collected as part of the ESRC *Making Your Way through Secondary School* Project (see above).

Barry Jones's fieldwork data: the quotation is from data collected as part of a QCA-funded project on *Boys' Performance and Modern Foreign Languages*.

Caroline Lanskey's fieldwork data: the quotations are from some exploratory interviews on pupils' views of responsibility in school post-transfer.

Jean Rudduck's fieldwork data: the quotations are from work carried out by a primary school as part of the *Thinking about Learning, Talking about Learning* Project (see above).

References

Adelman, C. and Carr, W. (1988) 'Whatever happened to action research?', paper presented at the British Educational Research Association Annual Conference, September, University of East Anglia.

Ahier, J., Beck, J. and Moore, R. (2003) *Graduate Citizens? Issues of Citizenship and Higher Education*, London: Routledge Falmer.

Anderman, E. M. and Maehr, M. L. (1994), 'Motivation and schooling in the middle grades', *Review of Educational Research*, 64, 2, 287–301.

Andersson, B. E. (1995) 'The contradictory school – a Swedish example', in B. Jonsson (ed.) *Studies on Youth and Schooling in Sweden*, Stockholm: Stockholm Institute of Education Press, pp. 19–39.

Apple, M. W. and Beane, J. A. (eds) (1999) *Democratic Schools: Lessons from the Chalk Face*, Buckingham: Open University Press.

Aries, P. (1962) *Centuries of Childhood*, London: Jonathan Cape.

Arnot, M., Reay, D. and Wang, B. (2001) 'Pupil consultation and the social conditions of learning'; paper given as part of the Consulting Pupils Network Project Symposium, BERA Annual Conference, University of Leeds, September.

Aronowitz, S. and Giroux, H. (1986) *Education Under Siege*, London: Routledge & Kegan Paul.

Assessment Reform Group (1999) *Assessment for Learning: Beyond the Black Box*, Cambridge: University of Cambridge School of Education.

Auden, W. H. (1939; collected in 1958 edition) 'In memory of W. B. Yeats', in *W. H. Auden*, Harmondsworth: Penguin, p. 67.

Austin, H., Dwyer, H. and Freebody, P. (2003) *Schooling the Child*, London: Routledge Falmer.

Ball, S. J. (1990) 'Management as moral technology', in S. J. Ball (ed.) *Foucault and Education*, London: Routledge, pp. 153–66.

Bastian, A., Fruchter, N., Gittell, M., Greer, C. and Haskins, K. (1985) *Choosing Equality: The Case for Democratic Schooling*, New York: New World Foundation.

Batty, J., Rudduck, J. and Wilson, E. (1999) 'What makes a good mentor? Who makes a good mentor? The views of year 8 mentees', *Educational Action Research*, 7, 3, 365–74.

Bearne, E. (2002) 'A good listening to: year 3 pupils talk about their learning', *Support for Learning*, (special issue ed. C. Roaf) 17, 3, 122–7.

Beynon, J. (1985) *Initial Encounters in the Secondary School*, Lewes: Falmer Press.

Blatchford, P. (1998) *Social Life in School: Pupils' Experience of Breaktime and Recess from 7 to 16 years*, London: Falmer Press.

Blishen, E. (1969) *The School That I'd Like*, Harmondsworth: Penguin.

Boaler, J., Wiliam, D. and Brown, M. (2000) 'Students' experiences of ability grouping: disaffection, polarisation and the construction of failure', *British Educational Research Journal*, 26, 5, 631–48.

Boren, M. E. (2001) *Student Resistance: A History of the Unruly Subject*, New York and London: Routledge.

Boyden, J. (1997) 'Childhood and the policy makers: a comparative perspective on the globalisation of childhood', in A. James and A. Prout. (eds) *Constructing and Reconstructing Childhood*, London: Falmer Press, pp. 216–29.

Bredeson, P. V. (1999) 'Paradoxes and possibilities: professional development and organisational learning in education', paper presented at the AERA Annual Conference, Montreal, April.

Bryson, N. (1990, reprinted 1995) *Looking at the Overlooked*, London: Reaktion Books.

Bucannan-Barrow, E. and Barrett, M. (1996) 'Primary school children's understanding of the school', *British Journal of Educational Psychology*, 66, 1, 33–7

Carr, W. (1986) 'Recent developments in teacher education', paper presented at a University of Ulster Conference on teacher research and INSET.

Carr, W. and Kemmis, S. (1986) *Becoming Critical: Education, Knowledge and Action Research*, London: Falmer.

Chaplain, R. (1996) '*Making a strategic withdrawal: disengagement and self-worth protection in male pupils*' in J. Rudduck, R. Chaplain and G. Wallace (eds) *School Improvement: What Can Pupils Tell Us?*, London: David Fulton, pp. 101–15.

Claxton, G. (2001) 'A flying start on a learning life: education for the age of uncertainty', *RSA Journal* 4, 4, 44–5.

Cook-Sather, A. (2002) 'Authorizing students' perspectives: towards trust, dialogue and change in education', *Educational Researcher*, 31, 4, 3–14.

Covington, M. V. (1992) *Making the Grade: A Self-Worth Perspective on Motivation and School Reform*, New York: Cambridge University Press.

Crick, B. (1990) 'Political education and the school', in *Encyclopaedia of Educational Research*, London: Routledge, pp. 72–81.

Crick, B. (1998) *Education for Citizenship and the Teaching of Democracy in Schools* (Final Report of the Advisory Group on Citizenship), London: QCA.

Cullingford, C. (1991) *The Inner World of the School: Children's Ideas about Schools*, London: Cassell.

Darling, J. (1994) *Child-centred Education and its Critics*, London: Paul Chapman.

David, M., Davies. J., Edwards, R., Reay, D. and Standing, K. (1997) 'Choice within constraints: mothers and schooling', *Gender and Education*, 9, 4, 397–410.

Davie, R. (1993) 'Listen to the child: a time for change', *The Psychologist*, June, 252–7.

Davies, J. and Brember, I. (1997) 'Did the SATs lower Year 2 children's self-esteem? A four-year cross-sectional study', *Research in Education*, No. 57, 1–11.

Davies, L. (1999) 'Researching democratic understanding in primary school', *Research in Education*, No. 61 May, pp. 39–48.

Delpit, L. D. (1988) 'The silenced dialogue: power and pedagogy in educating other people's children', *Harvard Educational Review*, 58, 280–98.

Demetriou, H., Goalen, P. and Rudduck, J. (2000) 'Academic performance, transfer, transition and friendship: listening to the student voice', *International Journal of Educational Research*, 33, 4, 425–41.

Dent, H. C. (1927) *The Secondary Schoolboy: The Nineteenth Century and After*, Vol. CI, February, pp. 208–16.

Dent, H. C. (1930) 'The aim: an educated democracy', *The Nineteenth Century and After*, Vol. CVII, January, pp. 10–16.

Dent, H. C. (1939) 'The adolescent's way of life', *The Hibbert Journal, a Quarterly Review of Religion, Theology, and Philosophy*, Vol. XXXVII, pp. 387–95.

Dixon, A. (2002) 'Sinking outside the box' (editorial), *Forum*, 44, 3, 93.

Doddington, C., Flutter, J. and Rudduck, J. (1999) *Improving Learning: The Pupils' Agenda*, Report for primary schools, Cambridge: Homerton College Research Unit.

Doddington, C. and Flutter, J. with Bearne, E. and Demetriou, H. (2001) *Sustaining Pupils' Progress at Year 3*, Cambridge: University of Cambridge Faculty of Education.

Doddington, C., Flutter, J. and Rudduck, J. (1998) 'Year 8: a suitable case for treatment', *Improving Schools*, 1, 3, 39–42.

Doddington, C., Flutter, J. and Rudduck, J. (1999) 'Exploring and explaining "dips" in motivation and performance in primary and secondary schooling', *Research in Education*, 61, 29–38.

Eckert, P., Goldman, S. and Wenger, E. (1996) *The School as a Community of Engaged Learners*, Institute for Research on Learning Report No. 17.101, Menlow Park, CA.

Edwards, B. (1974) *The Burston School Strike*, London: Lawrence & Wishart.

Edwards, J. and Hattam, R. (2000) 'Using students-as-researchers in educational research: beyond silenced voices', unpublished discussion paper for the Students Completing Schooling Project.

Engestrom, Y. (1995) 'Voice as communicative action', *Mind, Culture and Action*, 2, 3, 192–215.

Epstein, J. L. (1983) 'The influence of friends on achievement and affective outcomes', in J. L. Epstein and N. Karweit (eds) *Friends in School: Patterns of Selection and Influence in Secondary Schools*, London: Academic Press.

Erickson, S. and Shultz, J. (1992) 'Students' experience of curriculum', in *Handbook of Research on Curriculum*, ed. P. W. Jackson, New York City: Macmillan.

Fielding, M. (1997) 'Beyond school effectiveness and school improvement: lighting the slow fuse of possibility', *Curriculum Journal*, 8, 1, 7–27.

Fielding, M. (2002) 'Transformative approaches to student voice: theoretical underpinnings, recalcitrant realities', paper given at the BERA annual conference, University of Exeter.

Fielding, M. (2002a) 'The impact of impact: probing the presumptions of muscular change discourse', unpublished paper.

Fielding, M. and Rudduck, J. (2002) 'The transformative potential of student voice: confronting the power issues', paper given at the BERA annual conference, University of Exeter.

Flutter, J., Kershner, R. and Rudduck, J. (1998) *Thinking about Learning, Talking about Learning: The Effective Learning Project*, Cambridge: Cambridgeshire LEA.

Flutter, J., Rudduck, J., Addams, H., Johnson, M. and Maden M. (1999) *Improving Learning: The Pupils' Agenda*, report for secondary schools, Cambridge: Homerton Research Unit.

Franklin, A. and Franklin, B. (1996) 'Growing pains: The developing children's rights movement in the UK', in J. Pilcher and S. Wagg (eds) *Thatcher's Children? Politics, Childhood and Society in the 1980s and 1990s*, London: Falmer Press, pp. 94–113.

Freeman, D. (2001) *The Socio Political Construction of School Failure: Erehwon*, PhD thesis, University of Sheffield.

Freeman, M. D. A. (1983) *The Rights and the Wrongs of Children*, London, Frances Pinter.

Freeman, M. D. A. (1987) 'Taking children's rights seriously', *Children and Society*, 1, 4, 299–319.

Freeman, M. D. A. (1996) 'Children's education: a test case for best interests and autonomy', in R. Davie and D. Galloway (eds) *Listening to Children in Education*, London: David Fulton.

Freire, P. (1970) *Pedagogy of the Oppressed*, New York: Herder & Herder.

Frowe, I. (2001) 'Language and educational practice', *Cambridge Journal of Education*, 31, 1, 89–101.

Fullan, M. (1991) *The New Meaning of Educational Change*, New York: Teachers' College Press.

Fullan, M. and Watson, N. (2000) 'School-based management: reconceptualising to improve learning outcomes', in *School Effectiveness and School Improvement*, 11, 4, 453–73.

Galncey, J. (1998) 'Back to the future with Dome of the seventies', the *Guardian*, 25 February.

Galton, M., Gray, J. and Rudduck, J. (2003) *Transfer and Transvisions in the Middle Years of Schooling (7–14): Continuities and Discontinuities in Learning*, Final Report to the DfES.

Gilbert, R. N. and Robins, M. (1998) *Welcome to Our World: Realities of High School Students*, California: Corwin Press, Inc.

Giroux, H. A. (1981) *Ideology, Culture and the Process of Schooling*, Lewes: Falmer Press.

Goodlad, J. I. (1984) *A Place Called School*, New York: McGraw-Hill.

Goodlad, S. (ed) (1998) *Mentoring and Tutoring by Students*, London: Kogan Page.

Grace, G. (1995) *School Leadership*, London, Falmer Press.

Gray, J. M. (1990) 'The quality of schooling: frameworks for judgment', *British Journal of Educational Studies*, 38, 3, 204–33.

Greene, M. (1985) 'Teacher as project: choice, perspective and the public space', quoted by J. Smyth (1987) 'Transforming teaching through intellectualising the work of teachers', in J. Smyth (ed.) *Educating Teachers*, Lewes: Falmer Press, pp. 155–68.

Hall, N. and Martello, J. (1996) *Listening to Children Think*, London: Hodder & Stoughton.

Hare, D. (1989) 'Cycles of hope and despair', *Weekend Guardian*, June, pp. 3–4.

Hargreaves, D. (1967) *The Challenge for the Comprehensive School*, London: Routledge & Kegan Paul.

Harris, S. and Rudduck, J. (1993) 'Establishing the seriousness of learning', *British Journal of Educational Psychology*, Vol. 63 (part 2), 322–66.

Harris, S., Rudduck, J. and Wallace, G. (1994) '"School's great – apart from the lessons": students' early experiences of learning in secondary school', in M. Hughes (ed.) *Perceptions of Teaching and Learning*, Clevedon: Multilingual Matters, pp. 35–52.

Harris, S., Wallace, G. and Rudduck, J. (1995) '"It's not that I haven't learnt much. It's just that I don't really know what I'm doing": metacognition and secondary school students', *Research Papers in Education*, 10, 2, 134–53.

Hart, R. (1992) *Children's Participation: from Tokenism to Citizenship*, Innocenti Essays No. 4, France: UNICEF International Child Development Centre.

Hartup, W. W. (1996) 'Cooperation, close relationships and cognitive development', in W. M. Bulkowski, A. F. Newcomb and W. W. Hartup (eds) *The Company They Keep: Friendships in Childhood and Adolescence*, Cambridge: Cambridge University Press.

Hendrick, H. (1979) 'Constructions and reconstructions of British childhood: an interpretative survey, 1800 to the present', in A. James and A. Prout (eds) *Constructing and Reconstructung Childhood*, London: Falmer Press, pp. 34–62.

Hirsch, D. (1998) 'Schooling for the middle years: developments in Europe', follow-up paper to Hirsch, D. *Schooling for the Middle Years: Developments in Eight European Countries*, Washington DC: Carnegie Council on Adolescent Development.

Hobson, J. (1999) 'Tapping into a child's visual world reveals way forward for packaging', *Kids Marketing Report*, 27, January.

Hodgkin, R. (1998) 'Partnership with pupils', *Children UK* (summer).

Holden, C. and Clough, N. (eds) (1998) *Children as Citizens: Education for Participation*, London: Jessica Kingsley Publishers.

Holdsworth, R. (2001) *Youth Participation*, paper written for the ACT and SE NSW Regional Youth Services Conference, Bateman's Bay, October.

Holloway, S. L. and Valentine, G. (2003) *Cyberkids: Children in the Information Age*, London: Routledge Falmer.

Hughes, M. (2002) 'Homework and its contribution to learning', unpublished final report of an ESRC Project (No. R000237857).

Humphries, B. (1994) 'Empowerment and social research', in B. Humphries and C. Truman (eds) *Rethinking Social Research: Anti-Discriminatory Approaches in Research Methodology*, Aldershot: Avebury Press, pp. 185–204.

Jackson, S. and Scott, S. (1999) 'Risk, anxiety and the social construction of childhood', in D. Lupton (ed.) *Risk and Socio-Cultural Theory*, Cambridge: Cambridge University Press.

James, A. and Prout, A. (1997) 'Re-presenting childhood: time and transition in the study of childhood', in A. James and A. Prout (eds) *Constructing and Reconstructing Childhood*, London: Falmer Press, pp. ix–xvii; 230–50.

Jamieson, I. and Wikeley, F. (2000) 'School effectiveness and consistency', *School Effectiveness and School Improvement*, 11, 4, pp. 435–52.

Jerome, L. (2001) 'Teaching citizenship: from rhetoric to reality', *Education Today*, 51, 1, 8–12.

Jones, D. (1990) 'The genealogy of the urban schoolteacher', in S. J. Ball (ed.) *Foucault and Education*, London: Routledge, pp. 57–77.

Jones, G. (2002) *Diverging Paths to Adulthood*, report for the Rowntree Foundation, pp. 1–8.

Kenway, J. and Bullen, E. (2001) *Consuming Children*, Buckingham: Open University Press.

Kozol, J. (1991) *Savage Inequalities: Children in America's Schools*, New York City: Harper Perennial.

Kvalsund, R. (2000) 'The transition from primary to secondary level in smaller and larger rural schools in Norway', *International Journal of Educational Research*, 33, 4, 401–24.

Lacey, C. (1970) *Hightown Grammar: The School as a Social System*, Manchester: Manchester University Press.

Ladd, G. W. (1990) 'Having friends, keeping friends, making friends, and being liked by peers in the classroom: predictors of children's early school adjustment?', *Child Development*, 61, 1081–100.

Lampert, M. (2000) 'Knowing teaching: the intersection of research on teaching and qualitative research', *Harvard Educational Review*, 70, 1, 86–99.

Lansdown, G. (1994) 'Children's rights', in B. Mayall (ed.) *Children's Childhoods: Observed and Experienced*, London: Falmer Press, pp. 33–44.

Lanskey, C., Rudduck, J. and Arnot, M. (2002) 'Student consultation, community and the democratic tradition', paper given at the AERA Annual Conference, New Orleans, April.

Larsen, J. (2001) *Contestations, Innovations and Change: A Case Study of a New Western Australian Secondary School*, PhD thesis, University of London, Institute of Education.

Lawton, D. (2001) *The Future of the School Curriculum in the 21st Century*, Occasional Paper 14, UCET.

Levin, B. (1995) 'Improving educational productivity through a focus on learners', *International Studies in Educational Administration*, 60, 15–21.

Levin, B. (1998) 'The educational requirement for democracy', *Curriculum Inquiry*, 28, 1, 57–79.

Levin, B. (1999) 'Putting students at the centre in education reform', unpublished paper.

Levine, J. M. and Wang, M. C. (eds) (1983) *Teacher and Student Perceptions: Implications for Learning*, Hillsdale, NJ: Lawrence Erlbaum Associates.

Louis, K. S. and Miles, M. B. (1990) *Improving the Urban High School: What Works and Why*, London: Cassell.

Lucey, H. and Reay, D (1999) 'First choice or second best? The impact on children of not getting their first choice of secondary school', paper presented at the annual conference of the British Educational Research Association, September.

MacBeath, J., Demetriou, H., Rudduck, J. and Myers, K. (2003) *Consulting Pupils: A Toolkit for Teachers*, Cambridge: Pearson Publishing.

MacBeath, J., Schratz, M., Meuret, D. and Jakobsen, L. (2000), *Self-Evaluation in European Schools, A Story of Change*, London: Routledge Falmer.

MacBeath, J. and Sugimine, H. (2003) *Self-Evaluation in the Global Classroom*, London: Routledge Falmer.

MacBeath, J. and McGlynn, A. (2002) *Self-Evaluation: What's in it for Schools?*, London: Routledge Falmer.

MacBeath, J. and Weir, D. (1991) *Attitudes to School*, Glasgow: Jordanhill College.

McGregor, J. (2002) 'Making spaces: teacher workplace topologies', unpublished paper, National College for School Leadership.

MacIntyre, D. and Pedder, D. (in press) 'The impact of pupil consultation on classroom practice', in M. Arnot, D. McIntyre, D. Pedder and D. Reay, *Consultation in the Classroom*, Cambridge: Pearson Publishing.

MacNeice, L. (1950) 'Snow', in K. Allott (ed.) *The Penguin Book of Contemporary Verse*, Harmondsworth: Penguin Books.

Mayall, B. (1994): 'Introduction', in B. Mayall (ed.) *Children's Childhoods Observed and Experienced*, London: Falmer Press, pp. 1–12.

Meadmore, S. D. (1993) 'The production of individuality through examination', *British Journal of Sociology of Education*, 14, 1, 59–73.

Measor, L. and Woods, P. (1984) *Changing Schools*, Milton Keynes: Open University Press.

Mitchell, C. and Sackney, L. (2000) *Profound Improvement: Building Capacity for a Learning Community*, Netherlands: Swets & Zeitlinger.

Mitra, D. (2001) 'Going to the source: student voice in high school reform', paper presented at the annual conference of the American Educational Research Association, Seattle, Washington (later version published in *Forum*, 43, 2, 91–4, summer 2001).

Morrison, I. (2000) '"School's great – apart from the lessons": sustaining the excitement of learning post-transfer', *Improving Schools*, 3, 1, 46–9.

Morrison, I., Everton, T. and Rudduck, J. with Cannie, J. and Strommen, L. (2000) 'Pupils helping other pupils with their learning: cross-age tutoring in a primary and secondary school', *Mentoring and Tutoring*, 8, 3, 187–200.

Morrow, V. (1994) 'Responsible children? Aspects of children's work and employment outside school in contemporary UK', in B. Mayall (ed.) *Children's Childhoods: Observed and Experienced*, London: Falmer Press, pp. 128–41.

Mullis, G. (2002) ' "Is this a good idea?" "It's a great idea" ', *Communicating* (Newsletter of the Consulting Pupils about Teaching and Learning Project), No. 6, September, pp. 2–3.

Murdoch, A. (1982) *Forty-Two Children and the Transfer to Secondary Education*, PhD thesis, University of East Anglia.

National Educational Research Forum (NERF) (2002) *Outline for Foresight in Education*, London.

Negrine, J. (2002) 'Order! Order! It's Headteacher's question time', *Communicating* (Newsletter of the Consulting Pupils about Teaching and Learning Project), No. 7, November, p. 4.

Neill, A. S. (1917) *A Dominie's Log*, London: Herbert Jenkins Ltd.

Newcomb, A. F., and Brady, J. E. (1982) 'Mutuality in boys' friendship relations', *Child Development*, 53, 392–5.

Newman, E. (1997) 'Children's views of school: a vehicle for developing teaching practice', unpublished paper, Faculty of Education, University of the West of England.

Nieto, S. (1994) 'Lessons from students on creating a chance to dream', *Harvard Educational Review*, 64, 4, 392–426.

Nisbet, J. D. and Entwistle, N. J. (1969) *The Transition to Secondary School*, London: London University Press.

Nixon, J., Martin, J., McKeown, P. O. and Ranson, S. (1996) *Encouraging Learning*, Buckingham: Open University Press.

Nucifora, A. (2000) 'Advertising age: generation Y bears watching in marketing mix', *Houston Business Journal*, 30, 44.

Oakley, A. (1994) 'Women and children first and last: parallels and differences between children's and women's studies', in B. Mayall (ed.) *Children's Childhoods: Observed and Experienced*, London: Falmer Press, pp. 13–32.

Ofsted (1999) *Standards and Quality in Education 1997/98*, annual report of Her Majesty's Chief Inspector of Schools, London: HMSO.

O'Neill, O. (2002) *A Question of Trust* (The Reith Lectures), Cambridge: Cambridge University Press.

Osborne, J. F and Collins, S. (1999) 'Are you ready to blast off?', *Times Educational Supplement*, in *Science and Technology Supplement*, 31 December.

Osler, A. (1994) 'The UN Convention on the Rights of the Child: some implications for teacher education', *Educational Review*, 46, 2, 141–50.

Osterman, K. F. (2000), 'Students' need for belonging in the school community', *Review of Educational Research*, 2000, 70, 3, 323–67.

Page, R. (1989) 'The lower track curriculum at a "heavenly" high school: Cycles of prejudice', *Journal of Curriculum Studies*, 21, 3, 197–221.

Paley, V. G., (1986) 'On listening to what the children say', *Harvard Educational Review*, 56, 2, 122–31.

Pedder, D. and McIntyre, D. (2001) *Consulting Pupils: Some constraints*, paper presented to the TLRP Annual Conference, University of Birmingham, November.

Phelan, P., Locke Davidson, A., Cao Yu, H. (1991) 'Students' multiple worlds: negotiating the boundaries of family, peer, and school cultures', *Anthropology and Education Quarterly*, 22, 3, 224–50.

Pietarinen, J. (2000) 'Transfer to and study at secondary school in Finnish school culture: developing schools on the basis of pupils' experiences', *International Journal of Educational Research*, 33, 383–400.

Pollard, A. (1999) 'Towards a new perspective on children's learning?', *Education 3–13*, 27, 3, 56–60.

Pollard, A. and Filer, A. (1996) *The Social World of Pupils' Learning*, London: Cassell.

Power, C. and Cottrell, J. (1981) *Changes in Students in the Transition from Primary to Secondary School*, REDC Report No. 27, Canberra: Australian Government Publishing Service.

Prout, A. and James A. (1997) 'A new paradigm for the sociology of childhood? Provenance, promise and problems', in A. James and A. Prout (eds) *Constructing and Reconstructing Childhood*, London: Falmer Press, pp. 7–33

Putnam R. T. and Borko, H. (2000) 'What do new views of knowledge and thinking have to say about research on teacher learning?' *Educational Researcher*, 29, 1, 4–15.

Pyvis, D. (1992) 'Is youth policy really new?' *Youth Studies Australia*, 11, 1, 14–18.

Rachal, J. R. (1998) 'We'll never turn back: adult education and the struggle for citizenship in Mississippi's freedom summer', *American Educational Research Journal*, 35, 2, 167–98.

Ranson, S. (2000) 'Recognising the pedagogy of voice in a learning community', *Educational Management and Administration*, 28, 3, pp. 263–79

Rayner, P. (2001) 'A school working with Project 2', *Communicating* (Newsletter of the Consulting Pupils about Teaching and Learning Project), No. 1, May.

Read, H. (1958) *Education Through Art*, London: Faber & Faber.

Reay, D. and Arnot, M. (2002) 'Social inclusion, gender, class and community and secondary schooling', paper given at the BERA annual conference, University of Exeter.

Reay, D. and Ball, S. J. (1998) '"Making their minds up": family dynamics of school choice', *British Educational Research Journal*, 24, 4, 431–48.

Reay, D. and Ball, S. (1999) '"I'll be a nothing": structures, agency and the construction of identity through assessment', *British Educational Research Journal*, 25, 3, 343–54.

Reay, D. and Lucey, H. (2000) 'Children, school choice and social differences', *Educational Studies*, 26, 1, 83–100.

Richards, C. (2001) *School Inspections: A Re-Appraisal*, London: Philosophy of Education Society (Impact Series publications).

Rotter, J. B. (1966) 'Generalised expectancies for internal versus external control of reinforcement', *Psychological Monographs*, 80, 1, 609.

Rudduck, J. (1978) *Learning through Small Group Discussion*, Guildford: Society for Research into Higher Education.

Rudduck, J. (1991) *Innovation and Change: Developing Involvement and Understanding*, Milton Keynes: Open University Press.

Rudduck, J. (1998) 'Student voices and conditions of learning' in B. Karseth, S. Gudmundsdottir, and S. Hopmann, *Didaktikk: Tradisjon og Fornyelse, Festskrift til Bjorg Brandtzaeg Gundem*, Oslo: Universitet i Oslo, pp. 131–46.

Rudduck, J. (1999) '"Education for all, achievement for all": pupils who are "too good to drift"' (the second Harold Dent memorial lecture), *Education Today*, 49, 2, 3–11.

Rudduck, J. (2001) 'Students and school improvement: "Transcending the cramped conditions of the time"', *Improving Schools*, 4, 2, 7–16.

Rudduck, J. (in press) 'The transformative potential of consulting young people about teaching, learning and schooling', *Scottish Educational Review*.

Rudduck, J., Berry, M., Brown, N. and Hendy, L. with Chandler, M., Enright, P. and Godly, J. (2003) 'Learning about improvement by talking about improvement', *Improving Schools*, 5, 3, 34–45.

Rudduck, J., Chaplain, R. and Wallace, G. (1996) *School Improvement: What Can Pupils Tell Us?*, London: David Fulton.

Rudduck, J., Day, J. and Wallace, G. (1996a) 'The significance for school improvement of pupils' experiences of within-school transitions', *Curriculum*, 17, 3, 144–53.

Rudduck, J. and Flutter, J. (2000) 'Pupil participation and pupil perspective: "carving a new order of experience"', *Cambridge Journal of Education*, 30, 1, 75–89.

Rudduck, J. and Hopkins, D. (1984) *The Sixth Form and Libraries: Problems of Access to Knowledge*, Library and Information Research Report No. 24, Boston Spa: British Library.

Rudduck, J. and Morrison, I. (2001). 'Sutton Centre', in M. Maden (ed.) *Success against the Odds: Five Years On*, London: Routledge Falmer, pp. 275–306.

Rudduck, J. and Urquhart, I. (in press) 'Neglected aspects of transfer and transition: gender and the pupil voice', in B. Francis and C. Skelton (eds) *Boys and Girls in the Primary Classroom*, Buckingham: Open University Press.

Rudduck, J., Wallace, G. and Day, J. (2000) 'Students' voices: what can they tell us as partners in change?', in K. Stott and V. Trafford (eds) *Partnerships: Shaping the Future of Education*, London: Middlesex University Press, pp. 1–26.

Rudduck, J., Wilson, E. and Flutter, J. (1998) *Sustaining Pupils' Commitment to Learning: the Challenge of Year 8*, Cambridge: Homerton Publications.

Runkel, P. J. (1984) 'Maintaining diversity in schools', in D. Hopkins and M. Wideen (eds) *Alternative Perspectives on School Improvement*, Lewes: Falmer Press, pp. 167–87.

Sarason, S. B. (1991) *The Predictable Failure of Educational Reform*, San Francisco: Jossey Bass.

Save the Children Fund (1995) *Towards a Children's Agenda*, London: Save the Children Fund.

Schon, D. (1983) *The Reflective Practitioner*, London: Temple Smith.

School Works (2001) *School Works Toolkit*, London: School Works Ltd.

Seifert, J. (1983) *An Umbrella from Piccadilly* (trans. by E. Osers), London: London Magazine Editions.

Senge, P. M., Kleiner, A., Roberts, C., Ross, R., Roth, G. and Smith, B. (1999) *The Dance of Change: The Challenges to Sustaining Momentum in Learning Organisations*, New York: Doubleday.

Sergiovanni, T. (2000) *The Lifeworld of Leadership: Creating Culture, Community and Personal Meaning in our Schools*, San Francisco: Jossey-Bass.

Seymour, J., Cottam, H., Comely, G., Annesley, B. and Ligayah, S. (2001) *School Works*, London: School Works Ltd.

Shanahan, T. (1998) 'On the effectiveness and limitations of tutoring in reading', in P. D. Pearson and A. Iran-Nejad (eds) *Review of Research in Education*, Washington, American Educational Research Association, pp. 217–34.

Shaw, J. (1995) *Education, Gender and Anxiety*, London: Taylor & Francis.

Shultz, J. and Cook-Sather, A. (2001) *In Our Own Words: Students' Perspectives on School*, New York: Rowman & Littlefield.

Silberman, M. L. (1971) 'Discussion', in M. L. Silberman (ed.), *The Experience of Schooling*, New York: Holt, Rinehart & Winston.

Silva, E. (2001) '"Squeaky wheels and flat tires": a case study of students as reform participants', paper presented at the AERA Annual Conference, Seattle, Washington, April (later version published in *Forum*, 43, 2, 95–9, summer 2001).

Silver, H. and Silver, P. (1997) *Students: Changing Roles, Changing Lives*, Buckingham: Society for Research into Higher Education and Open University Press.

Smyth, J. and Hattam, R (2002) 'Early school leaving and the cultural geography of high schools', *British Educational Research Journal*, 28, 3, 376–94.

Soo Hoo, S. (1993) 'Students as partners in research and restructuring schools', *The Educational Forum*, 57, pp. 386–93, summer.

Southey, R. (1820) *The Life of Wesley*, London: Longman, Hurst, Rees, Orme & Brown.

Stake, R. E. (1995) *The Art of Case Study Research*, London: Sage.

Stenhouse, L. A. (1964) 'Aims or standards?', *Education for Teaching*, 64; reprinted as 'The concept of standards', in L. A. Stenhouse (1983) *Authority, Education and Emancipation*, London: Heinemann Educational Books, pp. 47–54.

Stenhouse, L. A. (1975) *An Introduction to Curriculum Development*, London: Heinemann Educational Books.

Stenhouse, L. A. (1975a) 'The aims of the secondary school', unpublished report, reprinted in L. A. Stenhouse (1983) *Authority, Education and Emancipation*, London: Heinemann Educational Books, pp. 153–5.

Stenhouse, L. A. (1979) 'Using research means doing research', in H. Dahl, A. Lysne and P. Rand (eds) *Pedagogikken Sokelys*, Oslo: Universitetsforlaget.

Stevenson, R. B. and Ellsworth, J. (1993) 'Dropouts and the silencing of critical voices', in L. Weiss and M. Fine (eds) *Beyond Silenced Voices: Class, Race and Gender in United States Schools*, New York: SUNY Press, pp. 259–71.

Tiemann, H. (1999) 'Heiko Tiemann', in *John Kobal Photographic Portrait Award '99*, London: National Portrait Gallery, p. 4.

Topping, K. J. (1988) *The Peer Tutoring Handbook*, London: Croom Helm.

Trafford, B. (1993) *Sharing Power in Schools: Raising Standards*, Ticknall: Education Now.

Tyack, D. and Tobin, W. (1990) 'The "grammar" of schooling: why has it been so hard to change?', *American Educational Research Journal*, 31, 3, 453–79.

United Nations Convention on the Rights of the Child (1989) UN General Assembly Resolution 44/25.

Urquhart, I. (2001) '"Walking on air"? Pupil voice and school choice', *Forum*, 43, 2, 83–6.

Wagg, S. (1996) '"Don't try to understand them": politics, childhood and the new education market', in J. Pilcher and S. Wagg (eds) *Thatcher's Children? Politics, Childhood and Society*, London: Routledge Falmer, pp. 8–28.

Wang, M. C. (1983) 'Development and consequences of students' sense of personal control', in J. M. Levine and M. C. Wang (eds) *Teacher and Student Perceptions: Implications for Learning*, Hillsdale, NJ: Lawrence Erlbaum Associates.

Warsley, P. A., Hampel, R. L. and Clark, R. W. (1997) *Kids and School Reform*, San Francisco: Jossey-Bass.

Waterhouse, S. (1992) *First Episodes: Pupil Careers in the Early Years of School*, Lewes: Falmer Press.

Watson, N. and Fullan, M. (1992) 'Beyond school–district–university partnerships', in M. Fullan and A. Hargreaves (eds) *Teacher Development and Educational Change*, Lewes: Falmer Press, pp. 213–42.

Wentzel, K. R. and Caldwell, K. (1977) 'Friendships, peer acceptance and group membership: relations to academic achievement in middle school', *Child Development*, 68, 1198–1209.

White, M. A. (1971) 'The view from the student's desk', in M. L. Silberman (ed.) *The Experience of Schooling*, New York: Holt, Rinehart & Winston, pp. 337–45.

Willis, P. (1977) *Learning to Labour: How Working Class Kids Get Working Class Jobs*, Farnborough: Saxon House.

Wolchover, J. (1998) Parent fury as schools reject record number of children, *Evening Standard*, 25 September.

Woodhead, C. (2002) *Class War*, London: Little Brown.

Woods, P. (1987) 'Becoming a junior: pupil development following transfer from infants', in A. Pollard (ed.) *Children and Their Primary Schools*, Lewes: Falmer Press.

Woods, P. (1980) *Pupil Strategies*, London: Croom Helm.

Woods, P. (1981) 'Strategies, commitment and identity', in L. Barton, and S. Walker (eds) *Schools, Teachers and Teaching*, Lewes: Falmer Press.

Wyness, M. G. (2000) *Contesting Childhood*, London and New York: Falmer Press.

Wyse, D. (2001) 'Felt tip pens and school councils: Children's participation rights in four English schools', *Children & Society*, 15, 209–18.

Index